Footballing Lives

Footballing Lives

*As seen by chaplains in the
beautiful game*

edited by
Jeffrey Heskins
and
Matt Baker

CANTERBURY
PRESS
Norwich

© The contributors 2006

First published in 2006 by the Canterbury Press Norwich
(a publishing imprint of Hymns Ancient & Modern Limited,
a registered charity)
9–17 St Alban's Place, London
N1 0NX

www.scm-canterburypress.co.uk

Second impression

The Authors have asserted their rights under the Copyright,
Designs and Patents Act, 1988, to be identified as the
Authors of this Work

British Library Cataloguing in Publication data

A catalogue record for this book is available
from the British Library

ISBN 1-85311-725-0/978-1-85311-725-1

Typeset by Regent Typesetting, London
Printed and bound in Great Britain by
William Clowes Ltd, Beccles, Suffolk

Dedicated in memory of Dave Langdon,
chaplain of Queens Park Rangers FC

Contents

Acknowledgements   ix
Foreword by John Motson   xi
Introduction by Arthur Cunningham   xiii
The contributors   xv

1   Who are you, who are you?   1
    Jeffrey Heskins, Charlton Athletic

2   We can see you sneaking in   14
    John Boyers, Manchester United

3   Shall we sing a song for you?   25
    Alan Comfort, Leyton Orient

4   By far the greatest team   39
    Phil Mason, Bolton Wanderers

5   No one likes us?   50
    Owen Beament, Millwall

6   With hope in your heart   62
    Bill Bygroves, Liverpool

7   You don't know what you're doing   68
    Roger Knight, Rushden & Diamonds

8   Who ate all the pies?   80
    Peter Amos, Barnsley

9   You only sing when you're winning   93
    Matt Baker, Charlton Athletic

10   Going down; going down; going down   105
    Chris Cullwick, York City

Contents

11 You're supposed to be at home   119
    Jeffrey Heskins, Charlton Athletic

12 You're not singing any more   134
    Matt Baker, Charlton Athletic

13 What's the SCORE?   148
    Ray Dupere, Watford and SCORE

14 Nowhere; you're always going nowhere   161
    Mary Vickers, SCORE

15 You'll never walk alone   175
    Jeffrey Heskins, Charlton Athletic

16 When the saints go marching in   192
    Matt Baker, Charlton Athletic

Postscript   198
Notes   199

Acknowledgements

One of the most nerve-wracking duties that traumatize most clergy and ministers is that of giving the vote of thanks at the end of a church do. Whether tired or exhilarated by the event's completion or success, the entire thing can be blighted by the omission of a single name. The success of almost any such project usually depends upon many more people than we know about, and the same is true of this project. There are some who we do want to name, but there are many more who have participated with a patience that would otherwise not be noted at all, let alone thanked were we not to do it here.

However, particular thanks must go to Christine Smith from the Canterbury Press who produced the seed of the idea for this book and cleverly planted it while Jeffrey was thinking about something else! It was a good idea and this compilation is the first of its kind as far as any of us know. Thanks too go to the football fanatics among her office staff who enthused about the possibilities of this book. We want to thank John Boyers who, over the years, has built up such a network of chaplaincy personnel that his was the obvious voice to listen to in selecting participants for the book. A project like this takes up a serious amount of time, and time spent on it, however pleasant, is time spent away from something else and so we also want to thank the contributors who have been both patient with us and punctual with their chapters. What this volume represents is a diversity of theological traditions and opinions. None of us would claim to be in agreement with every word that the others have written but all of us have been prepared to set out our stall alongside each other. Finally, we both want to thank those at Charlton

Athletic Football Club who have encouraged us in this project and those in our church communities, the members of Charlton and Blackheath Christian Fellowship and the parishioners of St Luke's and St Thomas's Charlton. Understanding that the time spent in putting something like this together is time spent in ministry to a wider community of people is not always easily or readily appreciated, but they have done so and we are both grateful to them for it and for their support.

Numerous people have commented on the chapters in draft and it was good to hear what they had to say, but of course the final responsibility for what has been written remains ours.

Finally, this book is dedicated to the memory of Dave Langdon, long-serving chaplain at Queens Park Rangers and a prospective contributor to this book before his unexpected death in January 2006. Dave was an inspiration and encouragement to many of us starting out in the world of football chaplaincy. While what is written on the pages here won't replace him, if it is an encouragement to others who are thinking about chaplaincy, then we think he would have approved.

Jeffrey Heskins
Matt Baker

Foreword

JOHN MOTSON

Over the years that I have been involved in reporting on life in the beautiful game it has become increasingly commonplace for me when I visit the League clubs to come across someone who introduces themselves as the club chaplain. One of the first that I remember was back in the late 1970s, about the time I commentated on my first Cup Final for the BBC, when I came across the Revd John Boyers running around the track of the Watford training ground with the players. John was among the few who were pioneering chaplaincy work with football clubs in those days and it is from those days that an entire chaplaincy phenomenon has sprung to life. When I last visited the chaplains at their annual conference in Lilleshall a few years ago the pioneering few had grown to a few hundred. Chaplains were there representing clubs at every level of the game. Premier League clubs, semi-professional sides and small clubs from the amateur leagues all had men (and one or two women in some cases) representing them in the officially adopted capacity of club chaplain.

It was my Dad, the Revd William Motson, who really introduced me to football when he was first the minister of Plumstead Methodist Church in South East London and later as the Superintendent Minister of the Deptford Mission. In those years, I found my passion for the game at Charlton's Valley and the Lions' Den in Millwall, and it has served my appetite and love for the game wherever I have found it well represented ever since. But I also learned from my father's work, and those early days when football clubs were richly identified with the communities that surrounded them. Those days in Plumstead and Lewisham, and later in the East End Mission of Stepney where my family moved to, were good examples of that. They could be tough old places, but in those days human values were important and people seemed to know what it was to live as a community. I saw this again at Watford FC where, as I have indicated elsewhere, there was a club that never forgot its roots in the local community, and, when I met him, their club chaplain personified this with his down-to-earth, honest and affable character.[1]

I have had cause to think a fair bit about chaplains in sport generally and football in particular ever since I first came across Christians in Sport when I was at Radio 2 in the late 1960s (before the days of Five Live). Few would deny that the face of the modern game has changed immensely. While it remains hugely entertaining, it brings with it pressures to players and others that most of us cannot begin to imagine. Winning has become all important; we are the champions – no time for losers, as the song goes, and I think that what is lost with all of that is a sense of perspective on life, which is a great shame. It is for that reason that I welcome *Footballing Lives*. Here in this book is a look at the game and those involved in it from the viewpoint of a group of men and women who have found their way into it and offer us the chance to regain that sense of perspective and ask the important questions of life again. To that extent it is different from other books about the world of football. The contributors are almost unique to the clubs they serve. They are accountable to their clubs but not paid by them. They offer time and some professional expertise and know the value of keeping confidences, which in a world where the leaked story and the dropping of names is commonplace is a value recovered. Sometimes they get asked to do the kind of tasks that most of us would never care to face. Here in the chapters of this book we have a glimpse of some of the issues that never make the back pages. Yet they are important because they are real. I am glad that some of the scepticism that greeted chaplains in their formative years (and there was some) has given way to a quiet acknowledgement that there is a place for the personal touch in what might otherwise be an impersonal footballing world. What this book does is to give a small insight into some of that. I hope you enjoy reading it.

Introduction

ARTHUR CUNNINGHAM

'What has religion got to do with football?' is a question I have often been asked by quizzical and bemused radio commentators (not John Motson I hasten to add!). This is an understandable question because the Church has moved over the years from being at the centre of public life, which was the case a few generations ago, to the reality today where it is very often viewed as being peripheral in community life and, indeed, is generally regarded by many people as being irrelevant and outdated.

However, I often reverse the question posed by interviewers by responding with the robust rejoinder, 'What has football got to do with religion?' And the answer is a great deal. It is interesting to note that a number of football clubs owe their origin to various church groups – as well as factories, mines and other community groups. For example, both Aston Villa and Birmingham City were founded by cricket enthusiasts drawn from local churches. In Scotland, Glasgow Celtic Football Club was established in 1888 by several Catholic parishes as a means of raising money to fund provision for poor children. In short, from the origins of the game, church members and clergy have been linked with football clubs in various capacities as directors, managers, players and supporters.

It is therefore not surprising that, in recent history, we have witnessed the emergence of the football chaplain (often referred to as 'Rev', 'Vicar' or 'Padre' at the clubs). Over the last thirty years, chaplaincy has developed significantly from a situation where one or two ministers were invited in to assist pastorally at the local football club to widespread involvement across all professional leagues today. Furthermore, such expansion has necessitated the creation of a charitable trust,

SCORE, to ensure professionalism and cohesion within this valuable ministry.

The role of a chaplain is a complex one. Most offer their services on a voluntary basis. Their primary function is to offer friendship, support and encouragement to their club and not to be presumptuous in offering comment on team affairs nor the running of the club. This pastoral ministry extends to directors, staff, players and supporters alike. It is important to note that this is not limited to those of the Christian faith but is also available to people of all faiths or indeed of no faith. The chaplain can also be a listening ear in times of trouble or crisis and this is undertaken with the proviso of complete confidentiality. For example, a player can be fully assured that anything shared with the chaplain will not find its way to the manager or directors of the club!

With this in mind, the reader will not find a catalogue of 'kiss-and-tell' stories within the pages of this book. Rather, I hope that you will be inspired by the accounts of professional and caring chaplaincy within the world of football.

The Contributors

Peter Amos is chaplain to Barnsley FC. He is proud to be a York-shireman, born just the right side of the border in Thornaby-on-Tees. A Middlesbrough supporter from childhood, he began playing competitive football at fourteen, selected simply because his father ran the team. Thirty-one years and one yellow card later (in his final game), he hung up his boots. Peter is a Baptist Minister in Doncaster. He is married to Jean, has four beautiful daughters (all of whom share his passion for football) and seven delightful grandchildren. Peter also has an interest in endurance and adrenaline-based sports, but his biggest rush comes from his personal relationship with Jesus.

Matt Baker was born in Kent but ever since he can remember has lived in London. He is a lifelong Charlton fan in a family of Charlton supporters that has now spanned four generations. He studied Law at City of London Polytechnic and went on to qualify as a solicitor. In 1993 he left the law to pursue theological training at Spurgeon's College and became a leader of Charlton and Blackheath Christian Fellowship where he is still based. Matt has been co-chaplain at Charlton Athletic since 2000 and is also a trustee of SCORE. He is married to Helen and has two children.

Owen Beament was brought up in early days with homes in Aden, Addis Ababa, Oxford and London. Since the early 1960s his home has been South East London. He trained for the ministry at Bishop's College Cheshunt, Cane Hill Psychiatric Hospital and the Saracens Rugby Club. He is currently Vicar of All Saints New Cross, where he has been for 31 years. He is married with one son. In 2001 he was awarded an MBE for services to the community of Deptford and New Cross. He is chaplain to Millwall FC.

John Boyers was born in 1949, in Grimsby, Lincolnshire. After training as a teacher he was ordained as a Baptist minister in 1979, serving a church in Watford and becoming chaplain to Watford FC. In 1991 he began to pioneer the development of chaplaincy in sport, under the auspices of SCORE, a newly established registered charity. In 1992 he became chaplain to Manchester United FC, while remaining National Director of SCORE. He has spoken at various conferences worldwide and has been involved in chaplaincy at some major sports events including world cross-country finals, ABA boxing finals, Rugby League World Cup finals, Commonwealth Games, Olympics and Paralympics. He and his wife Anne, a teacher, were married in 1972, and have two children, Andrew and Jonathan.

Bill Bygroves has been the pastor at Bridge Chapel in Liverpool for 25 years and has seen the work grow significantly in that time. He has had long-standing involvement with Liverpool FC in a number of different roles: academy coach, community co-ordinator and as club chaplain. He is married to Dot and they have four grown-up children.

Alan Comfort started out as your typical professional footballer. He was brought up in the ordinary surroundings of Aldershot where a rare gift for playing football emerged. After playing for QPR, Cambridge United, Leyton Orient and lastly Middlesbrough, his career was tragically cut short by a knee injury. However, his story is not your typical footballer's story. After a dramatic conversion to Christianity at the age of twenty, he actively lived out this faith in the world of professional football before training to become a Church of England vicar after his injury. He is presently Vicar of St Mary's Loughton and married to Jill with three children. He has been chaplain of Leyton Orient for the past 11 years.

Chris Cullwick grew up in Swindon. He gained a first in geography at Hull and a diploma in careers counselling at Reading before working in the careers service in Nottingham. Chris read theology at Wycliffe Hall, Oxford. Ordained in 1981, he returned to Nottingham for a first curacy before joining the staff at St Michael le Belfrey in York. Still in York more than twenty years later he now works full time for York Workplace Chaplaincy, a role which includes chaplaincy to York City FC. He is married to Joy and has two grown sons.

Arthur Cunningham was born in Doncaster. He is an Anglican minister having served in parishes in London, Somerset, Worcestershire and Greater Manchester. He is presently Vicar of Leigh in Lancashire and is currently chaplain to the Mayor of Wigan and also chaplain to Leigh Rugby League FC. He pioneered the development of chaplaincy at Yeovil FC in the 1990s and serves as the Chair of Trustees and Management Committee of SCORE. Arthur is married to Elizabeth, a solicitor, and they have four children, two cats and a goldfish!

Ray Dupere was born in Georgia and grew up on military bases in the USA and overseas. He graduated from the US Military Academy and served in the army for a time before leaving to study at Dallas Theological Seminary. He subsequently pastored in Hampden, Mail for 18 years and retired as a full colonel from the US Army National Guard Chaplains Corps. He now lives and works in Watford for SCORE, and is also the chaplain of Watford FC. He is married to Avril and has two grown children.

Jeffrey Heskins was born in Australia before being transported to England where he grew up and went to school in Canterbury, Kent. He read theology at King's College, London and was ordained in London where he has spent the rest of his working life to date. He has been a curate in Hampstead, a youth training officer in Enfield, a vicar in Kidbrooke and is now Rector of the parishes of St Luke and St Thomas, Charlton, where he is also co-chaplain with Matt Baker to Charlton Athletic FC. He is married to Rachel and has three children.

Roger Knight was born in Bournemouth where he worked as a trainee accountant before training to be a teacher. He trained for the ordained ministry at Lincoln Theological College. After ordination in Bristol Cathedral he was a curate in Hartcliffe before moving to Peterborough diocese serving as Vicar of Naseby, Team Rector in Corby, Rector of Irthlingborough and then of Burton Latimer. Roger has been a football referee since 1957 and has been chaplain of Rushden & Diamonds FC since 1994. Now retired, he lives within walking distance of Nene Park where he is a member of the Supporters' Trust Board which runs the club. In 1992 he was made an honorary canon of Peterborough Cathedral. He has been married to Ann since 1965 and has two children and three grandchildren.

Phil Mason was born in Preston and went on to study theology at Westminster College, Oxford. He trained for the Methodist ministry at Manchester and studied social and pastoral theology. He is married to Alyson with four children. He is currently serving as Methodist Superintendent Minister in Bolton Methodist Mission within the town centre. He is very involved in the life of the town and in local commercial radio, as well as being the chaplain to Bolton Wanderers.

Mary Vickers was born in Devon but moved to Liverpool when she was eight years old. She remained there until beginning ministerial training in Nottingham, and learned much about following football if not about the game itself. Since leaving theological college in 1985, she has worked in parishes, in world mission education and in chaplaincy in various contexts – hospitals, the retail trade, local government, the armed forces and now sport. In 2004, she was part of the international, ecumenical and multifaith chaplaincy team based in the Athletes' Village for the Olympic Games in Athens. Chaplaincy at Royal Ascot at York followed in 2005, when she also became SCORE's Chaplaincy Co-ordinator for Women in Sport. She is married to Peter, who is also an Anglican priest working in chaplaincy.

1. Who are you, who are you?

JEFFREY HESKINS
Charlton Athletic

> I was the only Arsenal supporter in the first year. QPR, the nearest First Division team, had Rodney Marsh; Chelsea had Peter Osgood, Tottenham had Greaves . . . [b]ut in that glorious first football-saturated term, it didn't matter that I was on my own. In our dormitory town no club had a monopoly on support . . . [t]he main thing was that you were a believer.[1]

There are times when you come across a book that you simply lose yourself in. In writing his blurb for the cover of what has become Nick Hornby's footballing classic, *Fever Pitch*, Michael Palin reports that 'Good books about football could be counted on the teeth of Nobby Stiles' upper jaw . . .', all of which is true. What I find in trying to read this particular book is that I can never get very far without drifting away into a dreamy reminiscence of my own. Hornby describes his first Arsenal match, the penalty that Gordon Banks saves and the knock in off the rebound, and I am lost, cast back into a warm summer night somewhere in the mid 1960s watching the legendary Terry Paine torment the Newcastle United defence at The Dell. Southampton are playing in the Cup and my father, Hampshire born and bred, has taken me to the match. I can't see very much because the men are all so tall as they stand on the terraces and the first half I spend seated on the steps playing my own imaginary game, a fighting tournament with the dead matchsticks that are lying around courtesy of the numerous smokers puffing their way anxiously through the first half. I am rescued at half-time by a 'mother earth' woman who releases my father from his paternal responsibility to see that I have a good time and takes me to the front with the other children in her family. The Saints win 2–0 and there is a delirious feeling around the ground that is impossible to shake off. Even today, more than forty years later, I can smell the air and feel the excitement of a victory. Like many before and after me I had, without realizing it, fallen in love with what we have come to call the beautiful game. It is a love affair that has continued to this day. Like my father, and for no good reason of logic, I followed the fortunes of the Saints. Terry Paine, Ron Davies, Mike Channon were players that I defended to the death as a schoolboy. Martin Chivers was our record sale at £125,000 to the Spurs and a young boy called Shearer did quite well with us. It was one of the few things that cemented my relationship with Dad. Football gave us a common language, which we could choose to use, and a lot of silence that was never uncomfortable. Football was something that we did in company, never alone.

I think that is an insight that I have carried with me ever since. It is hard to do football or actively to follow football without engaging with others at some level or another. Sometimes that sense of community seems very artificial or fickle. Some of the fans who sit around me chanting 'I'm Charlton 'til I die' are the first to leave when the team is still losing with five minutes to go. But we are all back for more the following week, the errors and misfortunes of one game forgiven or forgotten by the next. There is a sense in which we are all believers at that level. Even the most unlikely occupant of the seated terraces returns each week believing that the genius they saw in the last game can be repeated, or that the appalling spectacle they last witnessed can never be seen again. There is no real logic to this attitude. It is part of a kind of faith language that all of us engage with at some implicit level, no matter how much we might tell ourselves that we are 'not particularly religious'! Like Hornby, I am a believer, and perhaps one reason why *Fever Pitch* counts as one of the great footballing books is that it filters all that is surreal and dreamlike in the beautiful game and doesn't prevent the believer from facing the real issues of life.

It is here that it departs from so much else that seeks to represent football. It is not *Roy of the Rovers* or even what has

become that cult classic *The Football Factory*.[2] It neither represents footballing heroes as ageless gods nor football supporters
as 'belching sub-humanity'.[3] Instead, it acknowledges that there
is a real human story to be told and that much of it is played out
in ritual, song and the telling – which is where all truly religious
activity begins. All of this is important since the alternative is
a lamentable and ultimately dissatisfying drift into evasion and
the inability to distinguish between reality and unreality. It is
easy to do and as a football chaplain I have first-hand experience. In the closest I have ever come to my fifteen minutes of
fame, I once appeared on *Match of the Day*. It could only have
been for about five seconds, but even my nephew in Australia
saw it. The marketing department at Charlton had just been
granted a licence to hold marriages at The Valley stadium. In
order to promote the new status, the department asked me if I
would assist them in a presentation at half-time during the following home game. Naturally, wanting to be helpful I agreed
and the following Saturday took my clergy kit in a carrying bag
to the game while sporting my red football shirt. I was to lead a
'bride and groom' on to the pitch while the announcer narrated
all the information about how you could arrange to get married at the club. At half-time I was admitted to the refreshment
lounge and directed to the men's WC to get changed. Emerging
in my clerical suit I went to meet the happy couple. Of course
they were not married at all, at least not to each other. They
were actors and the man playing the groom had only been married a few weeks before – to someone else. It was something of
a surprise to his wife when she tuned in to watch the game that
night! The bride and groom were having pictures taken in rather
contrasting surroundings to my changing facilities. We chatted together and agreed what we would do. At no point would
we say anything to suggest a wedding on the pitch (which isn't
possible anyway). Off we went around the stadium and across
the pitch bathed in sunshine with the away supporters chanting
nuptial advice that I do not care to repeat. We arrived at the
centre circle, had photographs taken and were about to make
our way back when the narrator with his roving microphone
thrust it at me and told me to pronounce them man and wife.
I had a frozen moment before delivering an alternative line and

quickly leading the 'couple' back. The away fans cleaned up their act and cheered as we passed them and we returned to our alternative changing facilities. I stepped out of clericals and back into my football supporters' shirt and, as I emerged from the men's room, one of the serving staff employed for the day looked at me and said, 'Oh! So you're not a real vicar then!' It felt like a parable of life where all that was not real was deemed to be reality and the one thing that was real was declared un-real. This is the risk we take in viewing the world of football. It is too easy to mistake the one for the other, and it might well be the reason why the number of good books about it could be counted on the teeth of Nobby Stiles' upper jaw!

There can be little doubt that the advent of the modern pro-fessional game has been driven by the world of economics and depicted by an uncritical media as a glamorous world of youth-ful success. That of itself is not a problem. What has become a problem is that because this seems to be the only significant image that it portrays, it presents a distorted image of the game and the people that are part of football clubs and communities up and down the country. It is a fantasy that is perpetuated in the likes of my favourite soap, *Dream Team*.[4] Every Sunday night my family settles down with takeaway pizza to worship at the shrine of the Dragon's Lair. Every Sunday night we can hardly believe the twists and turns that are the life and fortunes of Harchester United. What it seems to do well is to bring home the reality of the pressure of living in a world of competition and it raises issues that are pertinent to that world. But, hav-ing raised those issues, what it never seems to do is deal with them. So, one player is depicted with psychopathic tendencies, another with homosexual inclinations, another conducts an extra-marital affair one week and a different sexual relation-ship with a teenager the next, and one has a religious conversion and becomes a Christian. All of these issues of life are passed over for the drama of a suicide or a shoot-out in the chang-ing rooms. This is a world of virtual reality, but that is all it is. Beyond the glamour are the human faces that make up the real world. Living in that world is a marvellous place to be, but it is marvellous for different reasons. The Dream Team is just that, a dream (and quite often a nightmare!) because it never forces the question, 'Who are you and I in all of this?' What does follow-ing the fortunes of this football club tell me about my life in this community and the people that I share it with? 'Who are you, who are you, who are you, who are you?' The fans taunt players and each other with this question, but for a book like this, it is not a bad question to start with.

This is not a Dream Team type of book. You won't find a lot of glamour in it and there will be no kiss-and-tell stories or attempts at name-dropping. Instead, I hope that you will find it a book that has tried to earth itself in reality. Of course it is set in the world of football. The contributors are all chaplains to professional football clubs. Most, if not all, are engaged by the clubs they represent but are not employed by them; they are there because of a passion for the game and a desire to serve God and their communities through participating in the stories of those communities. Chaplaincy generally and football chap-laincy in particular has become the most extraordinary growth area in what are otherwise perceived as secular institutions. Whereas traditional churchgoing is reckoned to be in decline (by those who pursue such statistics), all sorts of institutions are looking to create chaplaincies. In the parish of Charlton I am currently, in addition to the football club, chaplain to a school and most recently to a local branch of a major supermarket chain. When approached by the latter to develop a chaplaincy, the organization that owned the store was actively pursuing a policy of placing chaplains in every store in the country. When I asked why they wanted a chaplain they were able to tell me that in those stores that had chaplains already in post, staff morale was higher than in stores where there were none. So what is it about the phenomena of chaplaincy or chaplains that sees them currently in vogue?

The word 'chaplain' has been with us a long time. It is de-rived from the word 'chapel' and was originally applied to the shrine built to preserve the cloak (which comes from the Latin word *cappa*) of St Martin of Tours as a holy relic. What hap-pened with time was that the derived word *cappella* came to be applied to the building that housed the holy piece rather than the cloak itself, and eventually evolved to mean a modest-sized place of worship; what we now term a chapel. The person who was authorized to look after the shrine was known as the *cappellanus* from which has evolved the word chaplain.[5] So in its original sense the role of chaplain might be seen as guarding the sacred to ensure its safety, well-being and perpetual existence. Left alone, this is a rather narrow definition, limiting the concept to one synonymous with an image of being God's bouncer! This clearly won't do. So we need to filter this understanding of chaplaincy through a rather more positive lens. Instead of seeing chaplaincy merely as an aspect of protectionism, I think we can distinguish three sub-images that emerge from the keeper of the shrine image.

Chaplains, unlike parish priests or church ministers, are not principally leaders of faith communities. The places in which they work are not established as a body of believers as such. However, as our root definition implies, chaplains are the guardians of something that they deem as valuable. Just as the shrine of St Martin was deemed valuable by the Frankish kings who set it up in the early centuries of Christendom, it was only of value if it could be shared with others who might benefit from it. So, Christians might come and pray in its presence for some cause or another, others might be moved to come to faith, and still others might simply see it as a place of safety where they could bring the secrets of their hearts. Chaplains then might be seen as people whose treasure of great worth is the time they have to spend. While most of us run through life using gadgets and doing things that we think are going to save us time, chaplains are people who teach us how to spend it. When most of us spend our day-to-day existence being actively busy, chaplains can be people who remind us that there is more to life than working all the hours that God made.

> The puritans practically worked themselves to death in the fields without getting much of anything in return for their hard efforts. They were actually starving until the wiser inhabitants of the land showed them a few things about working in harmony with the earth's rhythms. Now you plant; now you relax. Now you work the soil; now you leave it alone.[6]

I have to confess that I often find this the hardest aspect of chaplaincy life, but it is up there with the most significant. The treasure is the time you have to share when you have not demeaned its worth by filling up the day with meetings and all sorts of other distractions that prevent the visit from God in the human encounter. I never did understand the logo that runs 'Jesus is coming – look busy!' It seems to me such a contradiction of all that we aspire to in following the man from Nazareth. What is it that makes the difference? I think that it has something to do with the language that we use. In chaplaincy settings, since many if not most of those we are set among are probably not those espousing a faith, I find that explicit faith language often draws a blank. People become defensive or embarrassed. Yet it is an implicit faith language that they are ready and able to use. My supermarket claimed that staff morale was higher in stores where chaplains had been established. Morale is simply to do with boosting confidence. Football clubs thrive on confidence, and we need to remind ourselves that the very word 'confidence' means 'with faith'. From it we get words such as 'confidential' and 'confide'. The chaplain can be seen as a person of confidence because he or she is seen as one who can keep confidences. This is fundamental to exercising a pastoral ministry of any real credibility. If the treasure of great worth is the time that a chaplain can give in the context of the busy workplace or the cut and thrust of competition, the pastoral care that the chaplain offers will bring things of value out of those who seek out his or her time. They will be things that no one else will have time for, whatever the reason. They will often be things that the seeker dare not trust to another. However much they protest that they are not espousers of religious faith, they will understand the link between confidence and confidentiality.

The second sub-image that gives some description to the nature of chaplaincy is that of the clown. Some weeks ago, I attended a celebratory function at our club. As part of the security arrangements I was required to sign in and was given a name badge explaining who I was. As I pinned it to my lapel I took a second glance at it and noticed that the receptionist had written Jeff Heskins at the top of the badge and underneath had described me as CHAPLIN. It was a simple mistake and yet not a mistake at all. As an admirer of the great clown of the silent screen I found myself smiling that the chaplain should be seen as something of a Chaplin. Yet in one sense that is exactly what we are.

When I was an undergraduate I spent my middle year living in Dalston in the London Borough of Hackney. My best friend of those years and I lived in the caretaker's flat above the church hall at Holy Trinity Dalston. The church was quite unremarkable in that it was populated by a small but very faithful group of locals who turned out week by week for worship. But once a year it became the centre of media attention. It was the International Clowns Church, and at their annual service of thanksgiving, the clowns and the locals turned out in force along with television crews and newspaper reporters. It was a memorable spectacle and one that gave me a great appreciation for the image of the clown, particularly as I came to know some of them in the conversations that ensued. The vicar of the church, Michael Shrewsbury, was the first to challenge me with the image of the chaplain as comparable with the clown and I have been persuaded by his view ever since. My office at home is now littered with models of clown-like figures, each reminding me of my need for perspective when I start to take myself too seriously. Clowns, like chaplains, are not contributors to the national output, but they are commentators on life – or at least they are supposed to be. They are often perceived as fools and yet, historically, they have taken their place as a living paradox. So, for example, it is the fool in *King Lear* who is the only one in any position to cheer the old man when he is desperate in his rejection; yet he has also the wit to chide the one who has really been foolish – the King himself. Out of apparent folly come the words of wisdom.

Alistair Campbell reminds us that the fool is a particularly vulnerable figure to those who hold earthly power and that in the Christian scriptures we can find accounts of the apostle Paul being among the first to encounter this as he spreads the word.[7] When he debates with the philosophers in Athens they deride him by calling him a parrot and asking if he knows what he is talking about.[8] There is something of this vulnerability in the figure of Jesus as described to us in the synoptic Gospels. His style of teaching was in vivid contrast to those who taught around him; it elicited a simplicity that cut through the hypocritical nonsense that had grown up in some of the official teaching of his day. Curing on the Sabbath, touching and declaring untouchables clean, exercising an apparently positive discrimination towards foreigners (Samaritans in particular) and women and mad people. But perhaps the most powerful symbol of Jesus' vulnerability and the clearest depiction of him as the clown-like fool are to be found in the forced dressage of purple robe and crown of thorns most vividly described in the Fourth Gospel in which he is mocked as a king and scorned as a prophet.[9]

Campbell goes on to draw an analogy between the clown of the circus ring and the chaplain in the modern hospital. The insights he offers could quite easily be translated into any field of chaplaincy and particularly that of the chaplain at the football club. He refers to the work of Heije Faber and tells us that he sees the clown's role as containing three tensions. First, he (or she) is one of many circus acts and yet he has a certain uniqueness which sets him apart from the others. Second, he sometimes feels like an amateur in a world of professionals and what he does is often born of creative spontaneity, yet it requires study and training. Third, he tells us that to be truly a clown, the clown must never seem quite at home in the circus.[10]

It doesn't take much to translate this imagery to the world of chaplaincy and to the chaplain. Simplicity, spontaneity and the desire to be seen as different, risking being not quite understood in the longing to be valued, are the hallmarks of this ministry, and in it all a true sense of loyalty, being committed to living in the world, but perceived as not quite of it.

Finally, the chaplain, like the clown, must be ready to see the ever so slightly ridiculous in the self; the chaplain who cannot see this and live with it will probably not last for long. Laughter can be releasing or it can be cruel. There are those who use it in order to stave off the inevitable look at themselves. Laughing at others can be a deception in which we kid our self that what we see in the other is found nowhere in us. That is neither the task of the clown nor the chaplain. Laughter releases tension and what makes the fool vulnerable is precisely the commitment to refuse a part in such self-protection. The ability to see the faintly ridiculous in the self and to laugh at it is a way of celebrating our humanness. I am sure that it is a valuable tool of grace that will only enable the chaplain to be a truly prophetic voice in a world where there is too little of that kind of thing.

Woodbine Willie
They gave me this name like their nature,
Compacted of laughter and tears,
A sweet that was born of the bitter,
A joke that was torn from the years.[11]

During the First World War the concept of chaplaincy made a radical shift in the mindset of western Christian thinking. What had hitherto been perceived by many as a benign ministerial activity became changed by the vileness of this particular human conflict. Chaplains reinvented themselves, and the nature of modern chaplaincy was shaped by its activity in the most horrific context. It would seem to some that prior to the outbreak of war the role of the chaplain was understood as necessary to stamp out swearing and produce enough hymn books. It seems as though chaplains existed in order to send the rank and file into battle spiritually clean.[12] However, the recorded experience of Geoffrey Studdert Kennedy moved the concept of chaplaincy into an altogether different place. It seems as though 'Woodbine Willie', as he came to be known, implicitly understood the sub-image of the clown or fool for Christ. Much of his verse, written out of the direct experience of the war, is quite subversive and to that extent it is amazing that he ever got published in his lifetime. But where he breaks new ground is where he sets the chaplain (still something of a clown-like figure) alongside the men who have named that figure Woodbine Willie. Here we have a chaplain who is able to empathize with those he ministers to. Most often, all he can do is offer them a cigarette, but by being with them he shows a desire to understand who they are and what they feel. The remote, authoritarian chaplain figure of pre-war is transformed into one who enables changes in thinking and attitude to take place.

In the world of professional football, the one individual who has to make this transformation is the one who adopts the role of referee. I am amazed that football referees are not an endangered species. Sometimes I cannot imagine why anyone would want to be one; they remain the most isolated individuals on the field of play. I still remember taking my children to a game when they were quite small in which the decisions of one referee drew the attention of the crowd who began chanting at him. 'Dad, Dad,' called my eight-year-old to me, 'why are they singing, "the referee's a banker?"' 'I don't know, boy, but I think he works for Barclays,' I rather lamely replied. Mercifully I couldn't hear what he asked next because of the clamour of the crowd.

Referees are often seen as authority figures and as such they incite a variety of reactions. In an age where such figures in other institutions have had their authority challenged and subverted from the days where Pink Floyd told teachers to leave those kids alone,[13] football referees are finding the need to redefine themselves as much as chaplains. They need to see their authority as emanating from a different source. A good referee is generally reckoned to be one who enables the game of football to flow. He or she actually lets the game unfold and will interpret the regulations that are the safety and fair-play boundaries to that end. When this occurs the image of the referee as enabler is uppermost and it is in this image that the referee's authority is at its strongest.

When referees appear to be remote and punitive, they attract a good deal of criticism. In such instances it might be justified and necessary for their sake and for the sake of the game that they be challenged back into being enablers and interpreters of the games that they take charge of. No one likes an authority figure who leans on their authority simply to let everyone else know who they think is boss. Ordained ministers have been counting the cost of that particular insight for years. The Gospels contrast the authority of Jesus with that of the scribes and the Pharisees. Whenever the evangelists describe the authority of Jesus, they use the word *exousia*, which quite literally means 'emerging out of him'. This is quite different from an authority that is conferred by an institution. The authority of *exousia* is respected because not only does it allow things to happen, but it can be seen to happen. So what we are is described by what we do and what we do in turn somehow describes who we are. Studdert Kennedy learned that in the trenches. Every chaplain and referee needs to adopt that model. Nicholas Holtam, Vicar of St Martin-in-the-Fields (whom I remember as a very solid fullback in our theological faculty football team), describes this integration well.

> When I was training for ordination, I had a conversion. Some graffiti in a Cambridge lavatory read:
>
> > To be is to do – Descartes
> > To do is to be – Sartre
> > Do be do be do – Sinatra
>
> There and then I decided for Sinatra. For me being and doing are irrevocably intertwined.[14]

I really couldn't agree more.

The chaplain in this sense becomes a model of practical theology, which is what he or she really ought to be if we are to make any sense of the role at all. What do I mean by that? Quite simply this: at the centre of practical or pastoral theology is human experience based upon our practice in ministry. What the chaplain needs to do is exactly what Studdert Kennedy did with his verse, namely to experience the experience and spend time reflecting on it before considering what he or she might enable to happen next as a consequence of that experience. What might emerge is a new way of understanding God at work in the human person and in the ministry encounter. This certainly happened for Kennedy. The God of might and right who occupied the high ground of his thinking at the outbreak of war became transformed as God alongside in the midst of suffering and the human tragedy of the ugly conflict.

What follows now is a sequence of reflections made by chaplains who inhabit a different context from those in the armed forces of the First World War. To that extent they are unlikely to produce such dramatic images. However, I hope that they will offer insights into the world of professional football that few take time to consider. They will look at issues that are raised when things do not go well for players or clubs, how clubs and their chaplains deal with the wider community, what happens when a young player, full of hope, doesn't quite make the grade or takes early retirement through injury. They will ask questions raised by these issues and experiences. Where do chaplains fit into a context of competitive activity and how does faith make a difference for many in this world? In this chapter we have spent some time considering just what a chaplain might be in this context. In the next chapter we will look at how it all began and the things that were learned from the earliest days. Welcome to the book. Now meet some of the chaplains.

2. We can see you sneaking in

JOHN BOYERS
Manchester United

A church had invited me to do a 'special weekend' with them, with meetings for folk in the community, a five-a-side football event and Sunday services. I was chatting with one of the guests at the Saturday night dinner at which I was the speaker. 'It says here on the ticket that you are National Director of SCORE, a charity specializing in sports chaplaincy and chaplain to Manchester United Football Club. How did you get involved in all that?'

It is the same question I want to unpack in this chapter, so let me take you back to 1977 when I was a theological college student with a placement at a Baptist church in West Watford. I was a sort of YTS vicar, an apprentice minister, and St James Road Baptist Church was where I was learning about ministry practically, under the helpful and respected hand of their senior minister, the Revd Richard Harbour. My wife Anne was teaching in Watford – we had moved there in 1976 from Grimsby, where we had lived and worked (both as teachers) since our wedding in 1972. Grimsby was my home town; Grimsby Town FC, 'The Mariners', were my club, although I rarely had the chance to watch them in those days as I was often involved in coaching or refereeing sport on Saturdays, or indeed playing in one of the local Grimsby leagues. But please understand that, for me, football had meant the black and white stripes of 'The Town'.

Our move to Watford in response to a sense that God had called me to train for Christian ministry was a challenge in many ways. It involved getting behind a desk again instead of being in front of a class; it involved financial constraints as our income was cut by 60 per cent and our expenses increased! It also meant living a great distance from Blundell Park! But it also led to an opening which I never looked for, never even dreamed of – chaplaincy in football.

Mike Pusey, then a minister at Farnborough Baptist Church and still a valued friend, came to our Watford church one week-end in early September 1977 to talk to a meeting of our home-group leaders. We had 'home groups' in the church, meetings of perhaps eight to twelve people, to read and discuss the Bible's teaching, to pray, to support each other and to share Christian faith with others. These were led by lay people in the congregation and on a monthly basis Richard, the senior minister, and I would lead training meetings for the lay leaders and occasionally bring in a wise voice from outside – hence Mike Pusey's visit from Farnborough that September. In a coffee break Mike spoke with me about something which was to open a door for virtually all my subsequent ministry. 'Your church is very near Watford Football Club – have you ever thought of being chaplain there?'

'Never.'

'Well do think about it. I do chaplaincy work at Aldershot Football Club.'

There followed a sudden silence. What do you say to an established minister who confesses he's chaplain to Aldershot? Do you say 'Sorry', or 'Don't worry'? Mike interrupted my ticking brain. 'It's a really important involvement, both for the club and for me. There are people there who have no one to talk to, no one to help them when life's tragedies come along, like hospitalization, serious illness, bereavement, family troubles – and it's good for me as a Christian minister to get outside the life of the church, to meet people in the real world and to see their needs and listen to their questions. Think about it!'

The door was unlocked, but I didn't bother to open it immediately. My previous understanding of chaplaincy had come from my early Grimsby days in the family Methodist church. Some ministers had been linked to industrial chaplaincy on the south Humber Bank covering perhaps ten miles of large industrial complexes. There, a workforce of perhaps twenty thousand was chaplained by a minister for two and a half days per week – it seemed a drop in the ocean, or, more accurately, in the estuary.

About a month after Mike's visit, in the October half-term, the church put on a special week of activities for teens from the local area. We decorated our church hall and on different nights invited different Christian people, including a rock band, a drama group, a professional footballer, a social worker and a medic, to talk in a 'God slot', between low lights and loud music, about their faith in Jesus.

Our footballer was Alan West from Luton Town FC, which was quite a brave move for a Watford church! On the night in question I met Alan at the main church building and we turned left to walk two hundred yards down to the church hall. It was a Wednesday and to the right the floodlights of Watford FC beamed out to announce a reserve team match. Alan pointed them out, saying, 'You're not far at all from Vicarage Road, are you? Have you ever thought of chaplaincy at Watford FC? I tell you, we need chaplains in football. Just this weekend one of our players came to me to ask for help and prayer. You see, his dad was in hospital and he had just heard that he has cancer, there is no hope, it is terminal. He's got two or three months left. This player came to me to say he knew I was Christian, knew I believed in God and didn't know anyone else he could ask, but would I pray for his dad and all the family.' 'John,' said Alan West, 'you need to be involved at Watford FC to help people like that.'

The door opened a little more! Not pulled open by me, but pushed by Alan West. That conversation ate at me all evening, all the next day. I remember praying on the Thursday, 'Lord, if you really are saying something to me about chaplaincy at WFC, then please say it again as I don't wish to pursue this unless it really is you directing me.'

The next day God answered, in a remarkable way. It was Friday and as usual I bought the *Watford Observer* newspaper for 10p. I read the sports pages and checked on tables and fixtures for the local Hertfordshire league – I still played a bit at the weekend. Inside I became interested in a big article by Graham Taylor, the relatively new manager of Watford FC. That summer Elton John, the chairman, had tempted Graham to leave Lincoln City (where he had done really well in his first two and a half seasons of management) to come to Vicarage Road and build the club to take it up to Division One. Currently they sat about tenth in that old Division Four. But Graham Taylor had begun his revolution and the article that week was about 'community'. Graham, interviewed by local journalist Oliver Phillips, was explaining that he wanted the club to be part of the community. He'd spoken of taking players to schools, factories, hospitals etc. and then threw out a key line which hit me between the eyes – 'And if there are people in the local community who have particular experience to offer us, I'd love to hear from them.' Ding! Ding! Chaplaincy?

I felt, sensed and came alive with the thought that God had answered my prayer of the previous day. It wasn't something I'd looked for, or read into, but the whole thing had leapt off the page. There are times in my life when I feel that God has spoken to me. I believe God is a God who is great, glorious, majestic and high above all, yet is also one who reveals his ways and will to us. We can experience his general speaking to us through the scriptures and occasionally his specific directions, as a verse or a phrase becomes 'highlighted' by God's Spirit and speaks powerfully to us, confronting us personally. I do encourage folk to read the scriptures and to seek the word of the Lord as they do.

God also speaks in church services – in noise, in silence, in preaching, in praying – and he works in the world to speak to and through this creation. God longs to communicate with us. I'm saying that God is real, and though his being and his ways are way above all that we are, we nonetheless can experience his speaking, directing and calling.

And just as I look back to a time when I realized I was not a Christian in the way the New Testament speaks of being a Christian, and then sensed the need to respond personally to the offer of grace, love, mercy and peace that he makes through Jesus, here it was again. Just as I look back to several situations when I felt God was calling me to leave teaching and train for Christian ministry, here it was again. Once more, I sensed the 'Divine prompt'.

For me to seek God and his direction is a basic element of Christian life. Sometimes his way seems clear and his directions are plain; at other times his way comes to us by whatever means he chooses, even a phrase in a *Watford Observer* report. Sometimes his way is not easy to discern, but it's always vital to seek it out. End of sermon! So there I was, reading a paper with a strong conviction that God had really spoken to me again about chaplaincy at Watford FC. What do I do? Well, for a day or so, I prayed a bit more about it and thought a bit more about it. 'If this really is your will, Lord, I need to know how to proceed.'

I shared the idea with Richard, the senior minister at the church, when we met up for our weekly discussion times together. The motivation for football club chaplaincy work didn't come from some dreaming, frustrated football fan trying to find a niche in the game that dominated his life. Not at all! The motivation for it all was, from my viewpoint, from God. Richard and I talked much about the possibility and both agreed we should write to the manager at WFC, to talk about our proposal. Graham replied, giving us a date and time for a meeting, and on the said day we were shown to the manager's office. Vicarage Road ground then was nothing like it is now. Three basic stands – well, one basic stand and two far from basic stands – and mounds of grassy earth behind the corner flag quadrants told of a downtrodden basement club. And so did the manager's room when we went in. Some of you will know of Vicarage Road and the tunnel onto the pitch. In November 1977 the present changing-room corridor was then a corridor both to the changing rooms and beyond to an administrative/secretarial room, in which (yes, *in* which) was a manager's room.

Graham welcomed us, apologized for the old chair but said decoration and furnishings were not a main priority at the moment. We spoke of the value of chaplaincy – a pastoral and spiritual safety net; a support at times of crisis and difficulty; a professional presence when special services were needed; a listening ear, a totally trustworthy and confidential resource to staff and players; a help and encouragement to long-term injured, to young players just starting, to older players leaving the game, to the breadth of needs in office and administrative staff, and so on. Graham was sympathetic, but wanted to talk at board level about it – and, I fancy, give himself time to check us out.

Some weeks later we had another appointment, early in December 1977. He confirmed that we would be involved for a period 'to see how it works out' and invited immediate involvement until the end of the season. And what involvement! He wanted both of us to get to know the players by coming along to Monday morning 'easy loosener', a music-and-movement session at Watford YMCA. It was easy for players – 60 minutes of 'popmobility' – but not easy for us. I was 28 and fairly fit, so managed to cope, but Richard found it more arduous. But through those sessions we got to know the playing staff, just as at other times we met non-playing staff in their various offices.

There were several situations in that first season that called on our availability and very gradually both staff and players came to see the chaplains (Richard and I worked as co-chaplains) as being helpful and beneficial. At the end of our first season Graham Taylor invited us to do the same the next season, pronouncing the initial experiment a help and a success. At the end of the season 1978–79, I had finished my initial studies; I had been ordained as a Baptist minister and the Watford church had asked me to stay, taking on a full-time assistant minister's role. They designated one and a half days per week of my time to work as chaplain at Watford FC, as part of the church's commitment to ministry in their local community. Richard stepped back from his involvement as co-chaplain, perhaps with both thanks and regrets.

When Richard left the church four years later to lead a church in Didsbury, I was asked to become senior minister and yet still was given the fullest encouragement to spend those one and a half days of my time at Vicarage Road. What a generous and supportive church St James Road was in this initiative! Wouldn't it be great if other churches equally gave ministers time to work outside the church, in the real world, be it in sport or elsewhere?

Let me comment on my experiences in those early days of football club chaplaincy. I was not the first chaplain – certainly I was preceded by at least three other appointments. Clearly I was aware of Mike Pusey's Aldershot links, for he was the one who first raised the issue with me. As I talked with others in football, some were aware of John Jackson's links with Leeds United FC and later I heard of Jack Bingham's links with Stockport County FC. I am not aware that either was given the sort of encouragement I was afforded at Vicarage Road, where I became deeply involved with the staff, but the Leeds United experience in particular is interesting. Many players were aware of the help and support given by John Jackson, and when Jack Charlton left Leeds and took up management responsibilities at Middlesbrough he introduced chaplaincy there, asking Bill Hall to be involved in the 1980s.

The Watford model was a particularly accepted style of chaplaincy. The amount of involvement encouraged by the club and facilitated by the church enabled, over time, good, trusting relationships to be built between chaplain, staff and players. I still believe this is the heart of all good chaplaincy – a good trusting relationship between chaplain and the people at the club. My experience was that everyone was 'checking you out' early on, wondering just what you were about. I remember telling different people from all parts of the club how I saw my role – not a Bible-basher, not imposing my faith on people who didn't wish to know, but being a confidential friend offering pastoral and spiritual support. Some did ask deep spiritual questions wanting to know why I was a minister, why I chose to leave teaching, why I believed in God so personally, and so on. Others simply appreciated the care, help and support that were unconditionally, non-judgementally offered.

Anne and I were slowly accepted as part of the scene at Vicarage Road. We were invited to the club Christmas do, to the end-of-season awards night and to the chairman's summer staff garden party at his mansion in Old Windsor, all bonus involvement (which I didn't seek). I was asked to take family funerals of staff, to visit players in hospital and do the routine pastoral stuff that is the chaplain's normal work. Trust built up slowly, but over those first three years real acceptance began to grow.

From this I draw several observations. First, working where the people were working was important. I met them on their ground. With the players I was accepted in the changing room, joined in the twelve-minute run, the weight-room sessions, the circuit training, the cross-country, even five-a-side football at times. I was part of their world, and so with the office staff. When Adrian, a young accountant, died of cancer just a year or so after his marriage, I was able to help because Adrian and other office staff had come to know, trust and accept my presence in their world. Here is a principle straight from the gospel – John 1.1–18 – that of incarnational mission. Too often the Church wants people to come to it – a special service or event is publicized, and we ask people to come and join us. In the incarnational mission of Jesus, he leaves the glory of heaven for earth, to get his hands dirty – and nailed – for the sake of a needy humanity.

The Church perhaps needs to learn again that it has to release its ministers to work more in the world outside if we are really to follow this example. A second major observation is also based on the scripture passage in Philippians 2.1–11. I found that being a servant to people had phenomenal impact. Showing care at the bedside of a dying loved one; visiting a new player in their new Watford home to wish them well; sharing care and concern for the family about to have their first child; cutting the lawn of the guy who is away for four weeks over the summer and is concerned for his garden – these were all 'normal' chaplaincy things. All are examples of seeking to serve, to help, to support, to care. Some people just said thank you and others thought or asked why. Perhaps all Christian people should serve and love and care so much till the world they are in – the people at work, in their street, in their school, their family – also ask that question why. The world often seems a dark place, but Jesus' teaching says his disciples are to be the light that illuminates darkness. We are to do that in the world, by serving those around us.

The opening paragraph of this chapter referred to my current role as chaplain to Manchester United FC and I need to explain how the Graham Taylor era at Vicarage Road led to my involvement with the Alex Ferguson era at Old Trafford.

In the 1980s and '90s I was involved in visiting other clubs, sometimes to explain how chaplaincy at Watford FC worked and how, if the right person could be found, chaplaincy could work for them. In 1987, Ken Merrett, the newly appointed secretary at Manchester United FC, asked me to come up to chat about chaplaincy. Although offered a full-time role, I declined it and helped them find a local minister to function as I was doing at Vicarage Road. Our Watford church was growing, I was about to lose my assistant Chris Doig to a church in Peterborough, so it seemed the wrong time for me to move away. Moreover, if Manchester United were to appoint a chaplain, the model needed to be one that other clubs could follow. No one else would appoint a full-time, salaried chaplain, but many could see the benefit in an honorary link. Just as a few years earlier I somehow said no to Graham Taylor's enquiry about going with him to Aston Villa, I also said no to Ken Merrett in 1987. But God was doing things! I had increasing opportunities to talk about sports chaplaincy at conferences and subsequently became involved in some large events, not least the 1990 Commonwealth Games in Auckland, New Zealand.

When I was approached about taking the senior minister's position at a London suburban church in 1990, I chatted with my Baptist 'bishop' about the options. It was he, Roy Freestone, who urged me not to take *that* very nice opportunity, but to use my experience in sports chaplaincy full time. After much thought, prayer and discussion with leaders of the denomination, and many others, Anne and I concluded that here again was the call of God. In 1991 I left local church ministry and became employed by SCORE, a newly established ecumenical charity, to develop chaplaincy in sport. The very next year, Manchester United came asking again as their chaplain was about to stand down due to ministerial changes, so would I consider the post and role? We felt, after much thought and prayer, that this was God's call, so despite some major human reasons to decline, we agreed to move north. Our boys, then seven and ten and a half, were at last excited about Dad's job! When we asked their opinion, we explained we felt God wanted us to move to Manchester and for Dad to be chaplain of Manchester United.

'Will we get tickets?' asked Andrew.

'Probably,' I answered.

'Then we'd better do what God wants us to do!'

So we went north in September 1992 and since then I've tried to do at Manchester what I've always done since 1977 – in a sensitive, non-threatening way offer care and support to all sides of a football club. The platform of MUFC may have helped SCORE develop, but mainly chaplaincy has extended due to the valiant work week by week of chaplains around the country. At big clubs, small clubs, non-League clubs and Premier clubs, individuals give time to offer compassion and involvement, pastoral experience and spiritual expertise, and the word gets round.

To illustrate the point, the late Bertie Mee, who worked for some time as Graham Taylor's assistant at Watford FC, once spoke clearly to me of his support of chaplaincy. He felt if a club was to be 'professional' in its care and support of staff and players, then a chaplain to deal with the pastoral and spiritual needs was as important a part of the support structure as were specialist club doctors, physiotherapists, sports psychologists, dieticians, dentists, specialist surgeons, ophthalmologists, podiatrists etc. I found that comment so affirming.

I remember a few years ago, in mid-December, I went on Saturday morning to watch our under-19 youth side play Notts Forest under-19s at their West Bridgford academy ground. Our older son Andrew needed a lift back from university for Christmas, so the trip was convenient – and I do try to watch the younger players, usually at home, but about twice a season I follow them to an away match. That season, Forest under-19s away worked out perfectly. Some of the lads' parents were around and over the year had got to know me quite well. At the end of the match, two or three sets of parents came over to chat.

'Is it today, then?'

'Is what today?' I asked.

'Do they get to know today or this weekend? Do you know, Rev?'

'Sorry,' I said, 'I'm not sure I understand your questions. Can you explain?'

'Well, Rev,' said one father, 'we know the club could announce soon who is staying and who will be released and we thought if you, the Rev, are here, perhaps it will happen today. Perhaps you're here to help those who will be disappointed!'

One of the sad misconceptions is that the chaplain is relevant only if there is a crisis or disaster; but this isn't so and is taken up elsewhere in this book.

For me, relationships are key and the spiritual dimension impacts all areas of our lives, yet is so often ignored. Managers and coaches see a need to get the body right, the mind right and all know how social or emotional dysfunction can impair performance. In my experience, and that of other chaplains, it is the spiritual dimension that makes us become the people we are to be.[1]

Whether it is at Old Trafford or Vicarage Road, I've seen people, both staff and players (and sometimes fans too), appreciate the availability of a chaplain. Fifty years ago, everyone knew the local minister or priest and could call easily on their services when needed. In these post-Christian days, life still throws up its periods of crisis, where a spiritual dimension is needed, and quality chaplaincy offers this. Even at a club as big as MUFC, the care and concern for the whole person has led them to endorse and affirm the value of chaplaincy in sport. My experience at Manchester confirms everything I was able to pioneer all those years ago at Vicarage Road, Watford.

3. Shall we sing a song for you?

ALAN COMFORT
Leyton Orient

By the rivers of Babylon – there we sat down and we wept when we remembered Zion . . . for there our captors asked us for songs . . . but how can we sing the Lord's song in a strange land?[1]

My special relationship with Leyton Orient began early in 1986. I remember vividly driving down the M11 from Cambridge having just received a call from their manager Frank Clark. I was so excited to be heading home. Home was Aldershot and not London, but London had been where I played all of my early football, so home it was. As soon as I arrived at Brisbane Road I knew this was where God wanted me to be. I met Frank and he was keen to sign me. The deal was good but I would have signed even if it hadn't been. I wanted to play for Leyton Orient.

Leaving Cambridge United was not hard at this stage in my life, although in the beginning it had promised so much more. Just 16 months before, I had left the security of Queens Park Rangers to build a football career that needed some help to get started. After winning England Youth international caps and progressing steadily under the guidance of George Graham, my Youth Team coach and Terry Venables the Queens Park Rangers manager, they both left and I was surplus to requirements at the age of 19. Cambridge seemed as good a place as any to learn my trade as a professional footballer. It proved harder than I thought. By the time I left I was playing for my third manager in those 16 months. The club suffered relegation and the team was too young to cope with the pressures of failing. I played well at times and awfully at others. Being one of the top-paid players at the club meant that expectations were high, but I was still only 19!

Cambridge United was football suicide, but this was also the place of my greatest discovery: a Christian appointment. Up to this point in my life I had never entered a church building nor met a Christian who was willing to own this identity with any pride or credibility. Cambridge would change all this. Ironically, it was the player I was bought to replace who was a committed Christian. Graham Daniels shone for Jesus. Whatever pain he felt as his football career was decisively taken from him by me, the love of God overcame. He talked as if God was alive, as if God had a plan for his life. Jesus had died to change his life for ever. From this moment on, a light came on in my life and everything was different. I couldn't believe that God could love me that much.

I needed to know this because I didn't love or like myself at this stage of my life. No, I wasn't a depressive or from a difficult family background, I had simply made some monumental mistakes in my life that had hurt people and I couldn't get rid of the shame I felt. The first was getting caught shoplifting at the age of 14 and being put in a police cell in the centre of London. When the police phoned home, my mother was so shocked she climbed out of a window and ran. She never said anything to me but I knew how much I had hurt her.

The second was while I was playing for the England Youth Team in Norway. I stupidly went out one night when we weren't allowed and got caught. I was sent home in shame the next morning. Of course I was worried about George Graham and Terry Venables, but my mum and dad simply picked me up at the airport and took me home. They didn't say how disappointed they were, how I had shamed our family, they just took me home. I couldn't bear how I felt inside. I hated myself for disappointing them, even though they wouldn't tell me I had. Jesus died to take my sin and shame away. I felt like a weight had been lifted off me and it felt good. I was captivated by Jesus from that very moment. I wanted to find out all I could about him, I wanted to follow him. My life was never to be the same again.

Driving down the M11 towards Brisbane Road for that meeting with Frank Clark was like finding my way out of a maze. I felt like I had got so lost and just needed rescuing. My life had come alive when I made the decision to follow Jesus, but outwardly things had not been easy from that moment on. I guess many of us think that if God is on our side then everything will go well for us. God the lucky charm! Most Christians know this is not really true, but we still expect God to make everything right for us.

Everything was not rosy in the Comfort garden in the first year after I made this life-changing decision to follow Jesus. I remember going on a Christians in Sport weekend at St Aldate's in Oxford. I was full of enthusiasm because I loved God so much, but I remember Canon Michael Green interviewing me at one of the meetings. I had been a Christian for about four months. 'How's it going?' he asked. 'The team haven't won for 28 matches, I've been dropped from the side yet again, the elders at my church think God is about to take me out of football and put me in a "proper" profession, and my family think I've become a weirdo since I became a Christian. Apart from this, I'm doing well!'

They say things often have to get worse before they get better. There was one other major event that would take place before I could find my way out of the maze. The Cambridge manager near the end of my time there was a big character and an excellent motivator. He asked to see me in his office. I went and we discussed Christianity. I couldn't believe he wanted to know so much. He asked to see me the next day, but his reasons soon became apparent. Everyone else was more committed to the club than I was. They had to be because I had a day-release clause in my contract so I could go to college, and Sundays were for church. Everyone else would do what he said and when he said it. This was harsh because I hadn't let him down, but the crunch was soon to come. 'Who is more important to you,' he asked, 'God or me?' Such a conversation is hard to imagine, but it happened. I was stuck. My football career was everything I knew and I was on the verge of losing it. I said that God was more important to me. I was never welcomed back at the club again. He told me that no one would want to sign me because I was a fanatical Christian and he would make sure that any manager who enquired about me knew this. It felt like I was finished as a professional footballer. I left the club in a daze. Was he right? Did he have the power to end my football career? I was scared, but I didn't believe that he could stop God doing what God had planned for me.[2]

From the moment I walked onto the pitch at Brisbane Road I knew I was at home. Not only was I at peace with God, I had been given a club that made me feel at peace. I loved Orient from that first day and I continue to do so twenty years later. In my first game we drew 2–2 at home, but I played with a freedom and confidence that had left me during the long winter of Cambridge United. The next three and a half years would be very special indeed. The fans took to me immediately, the manager believed in me and the football team were winning matches. I was in heaven on earth.

The problem with doing well is that you wonder whether you can do the same at a higher level. I played well for Orient, so there was often talk of me signing for a higher-division club. Because of this there were times when I wondered why it didn't happen. What was I doing wrong? Maybe I just wasn't good enough? It's funny how as Christians we believe in our heads that God is in control and yet often forget this truth in our hearts. One of the bigger clubs had not come in to sign me because the time was not yet right in God's perfect plan for my life. If I had known then what I know now, I would have savoured every single moment of my time playing in an Orient shirt. These were wonderful footballing years and, equally important, very secure times for me to develop as a Christian. Good performances were regular and a number of goals followed.

The highlight of my time at Orient came in the 1988–89 season, my last for Orient. Every year, we just missed out on promotion but this was to be our year. We struggled early in the season, but after signing a very young Kevin Campbell on loan from Arsenal we hit top form. In the period of his loan, he scored eight goals for us, but his impact spread beyond his goals as I scored ten times during the same period. This was to be my most prolific year with a haul of nineteen goals by the end of the season. Promotion was finally secured through the lottery of the play-offs when first Scarborough and then Wrexham were narrowly overcome, with promotion achieved in front of a full Brisbane Road.

The life of a footballer can be very strange at times. As soon as the final whistle blew in that play-off final against Wrexham, I rushed off to catch a helicopter to Heathrow, a flight to Belfast, a small plane to Bangor and a police car to the church to be married at 5.30 p.m. on Saturday 3 June 1989. I never returned to Brisbane Road despite it being the most joyful of times. Success for football clubs is rare and must be savoured, but I had reached an unexpected place in my time at Orient. It was time to leave. The club made a half-hearted attempt to persuade me to sign a new contract, which devastated me at the time. However, the truth is that I needed to ply my skills at a higher level and if Orient had really tried to re-sign me I would probably have signed. God knows every last detail. He knows our personalities and I needed to be courageous and take a chance, I needed to trust that the time had come to step out in faith, but I needed a little push to do it. For many of the following months I yearned to be back at Brisbane Road where I was known and appreciated, where I felt safe.

For a person who was homesick living in Cambridge, the next footballing move might as well have been to another country. Jill and I returned from our honeymoon eager to know where God was taking us. It was to the North East, to Middlesbrough. It was a very long way from Guildford, and a daunting professional move. Middlesbrough had some great players. Gary Pallister was still there before his move to Manchester United. Tony Mowbray was the captain, Bernie Slaven Mister Middlesbrough and goal-scorer extraordinaire. All around me were players I had watched regularly on the TV and now I was training with them day by day and lining up with them on a Saturday. I had stepped up several levels and it was exciting and frightening all at the same time. I started in the same way I had for Orient. Twenty-five thousand people packed into Ayresome Park for the first home game of the season against Wolves. I dazzled in a 4–2 win and was off to a flier. The crowd sang my name and it felt like no other feeling

I had ever had. I could do it! In the next game away at Leeds, a goal down and in the second half, the keeper punched the ball out; I cushioned the ball with my chest then volleyed in off the bar. My first goal for Middlesbrough in front of a fierce Elland Road crowd – what excitement! I had arrived, the newspapers started to run stories about me and my faith in God and everything was happening all at once. God had blessed me beyond my wildest hopes and I was so thankful. After living in a hotel in Durham for nearly four months, we finally moved into a lovely house in a village just outside Durham called Shincliffe. At the same time we found out that Jill was pregnant and everything seemed to be falling into place. Our new life together was perfect.

Over the years I have met many people who are committed Christians. It has always been a mystery to me that some people can have lives that appear to be blessed from whatever angle you look, and others experience terrible suffering or struggles. We all realize that what we see outwardly is not always the truth of what people are experiencing. Some people appear to have very straightforward lives in God while others cannot hide a reality that is different. If God has a perfect plan for each of us, why do some Christians live lives that look so painful? Is this God's perfect plan? These are the sorts of questions that many people grapple with day by day. I guess I tried not to think about it while my life was going so well. I just thanked God and hoped that it would continue. My world, in our beautiful new home with my lovely new wife, was just about to cave in.

It was 3 November 1989. St James Park was the venue for another crunch derby match. Newcastle United away. In my short time in the North East I soon learnt how much these derby matches meant to the local people. This was my seventeenth game for Middlesbrough, but tragically it was to be my last. Halfway through the second half, with Boro 2–1 in front, I chased after a ball with the Newcastle number seven. We leant into each other, my studs caught in the ground, my knee twisted and I heard what sounded like a snap. As the crowd jeered I was stretchered from the pitch. This was to be the last time I would know the thrill of a professional football match. Within months it became clear that the cruciate ligament damage and associated knee problems were career-ending. I had missed no more than a handful of games through injury to this point in my career. I had played nearly two hundred and fifty competitive games but there would be no more.

I did trust God but this was not a pleasant period of my life. I knew that God would work everything out but my life was in freefall and I couldn't get control from any angle. I had no personal insurance against injury finishing my career, and the club hadn't insured me to cover what they had paid for me. The reality was that they were legally obliged to pay six months' salary. With this and a bit more, plus the Professional Football-ers Association payout for a player whose career is finished by injury, we had some money but it wasn't going to last very long. We suddenly needed to sell the house that we had lived in for such a short period. When Jill came out of hospital having given birth to Sarah, I had moved us from our lovely house to a rented house on the other side of Durham. These were desperate dark days in the Comfort house. It was so hard to accept that such a time is all part of God's perfect plan for us. If it was God's plan, then did he cause my injury? Did he cause all this sadness? Did he take away the one thing that I was good at? I never stopped loving God but I was very sad and down for a long time. I had lots of time on my hands and too many questions needing to be answered.

Two biblical characters and their stories spoke into my life at this time. The story of Job is a frightening story if we stop to think about it. Here was a man who lived a blameless life of faith. God allows Satan to strip away the things of value in Job's life until there is nothing left. However disturbing this story is, it shows Satan as the one who causes harm and God the one who allows it. As I reflected on what had happened to me, I felt more at ease with my tragedy if I viewed it in this way. Then there's the story of Joseph, whose brothers initially intended to kill him but then sell him into slavery at the very last moment. Joseph suffers greatly because of their actions but amazingly ends up as governor to the whole of Egypt. The story reaches its climax in Genesis 50.15–21 when Joseph and his brothers face up to the reality of what they have done. Joseph says those amazing words that have shaped the thinking of many who have suffered injustice:

> But Joseph said to them, 'Don't be afraid. Am I in the place of God? You intended to harm me, but God intended it for good to accomplish what is now being done, the saving of many lives.'[3]

However hard it was to understand why my football career had to come to an end, I knew that God would use this moment to work out his good purposes for my life.

My heart has always been set to serve God. Being a committed Christian in the world of professional football toughened me up with the constant banter and challenges to my faith from inside and outside the dressing room. I loved to talk about Jesus but suffered terrible fears of speaking in public. By his grace, God always helped me to get by, but the fear was quite overwhelming. When I realized that God was leading me into the Church of England ministry I was absolutely terrified. This has been a long walk of trust that continues to this very day. I was selected for ministry and started my training back in Cambridge (of all places) in 1991. It was a training that was completed in July 1994.

1994: return to Leyton Orient

It may surprise most people to hear that I had not returned to Brisbane Road since that play-off win against Wrexham in 1989. Understanding what a footballer's life is like is the key to understanding why I hadn't returned. The footballer's life is nomadic. You travel from club to club waiting to find one that both needs and appreciates you, knowing that as soon as you move on the club finds someone else to need and appreciate. As for other players, there's a saying: 'There are no friends in football.' It's not completely true, but very few make a conscious effort to keep in touch. This is part of the make-up of a footballer. I am still the same 15 years later.

God uses everything we experience for good. The depth of our insight into other people's lives forms as we experience life ourselves. All those years God was shaping me into the person I would become and in his majesty would position me in a place where I could best use the wisdom he was giving. Leyton Orient is the perfect place for me. What's more, God knows the world of professional football. Isn't this remarkable? He knows what makes footballers tick. He knows the discipline and self-sacrifice that most have to make to be able to live their dream. He knows how to reach into their world and speak their language. Let me give you an example. Most footballers know that the applause doesn't last. Appreciation is for a time and then the fans move on to another or turn against you. I discovered that God would feel the same about me no matter how well or badly I performed. In Jesus I saw the unchanging love of God that would always welcome and always rescue me. Such a message may mean very little to some, but it meant everything to me. The only life I knew was judged two or three times a week: six out of ten, seven out of ten, eight out of ten. Every week *Match* magazine would tell you how well you played. Every week the local newspapers would record your every mistake or success for thousands of people to read. How many other people have an average day at work and the whole of London knows? Very few of course. God doesn't produce a *Match* magazine. He loves us with a perfect love. Our sinfulness may disappoint him but that's why he sent his son Jesus to die on a cross on Calvary to wash us clean. The good news is that the first thing that Jesus will say to you is not 'Well played' or 'That wasn't one of your best games', but, 'I love you and there is nothing that you could do that would have made me want to die for you more.'

Over the past 11 years while being chaplain at Orient, I have become increasingly aware of character traits specific to football players. I guess I fit into the football world because of this, even if I am different due to my faith and clerical collar. Jealousy and insecurity are huge areas for footballers. Football is a team game, but you need to be in the team! The fear of a new player being brought in to replace you is never far away, so jealousy and insecurity rear their heads regularly. Perhaps the story of my arrival at Cambridge United can best describe this for us. On my very first day the manager John Ryan held a practice match. The team had been struggling and when I arrived it was obvious that a good number felt uneasy. At the time I didn't really understand why and thought them an unfriendly bunch, but later I realized it had everything to do with whose position in the team I was about to take. In the practice match I roamed rather than held one position. I had an inspired match, scoring and creating several goals. Graham Daniels played fantastically well also, and convinced himself that I would play in a different position to his. He later told me how reality hit like a sledgehammer when someone asked me what position I played and I said left-wing, his position. From that moment on, he knew that his career as a professional footballer was hanging by a thread.

We all crave security but the football world doesn't do security in any big way. In their desperation, players will try anything to bring them 'luck', to help them survive as long as they can. They need to know that everything will work out in the end – that they will be able to support their families, that they will find another profession after their football career ends, that they will be able to afford a home when they start again. For the Christian, such knowledge rolls off the pages of the Bible. Matthew 5 tells us that God knows our every need. He knows what we need to eat and when. He knows what we need to wear and to earn to be able to survive. He knows all these things, and the Bible tells us that just as the birds of the air receive all they need from a God who supplies for them, how much more can we trust God to supply our needs. If we are following Jesus then we can be absolutely certain that God will take us where he wants us to go, and give all that he wants us to have. He can be trusted!

A chaplaincy that has evolved

When I returned to Orient in 1994, Tony Wood was still the chairman. He welcomed me back as club chaplain without any real idea what a chaplain does. I was like the favourite son coming home and it didn't matter what I came to do. In 1995 the club changed hands, being bought by Barry Hearn, a well-known boxing and snooker promoter, for £5. His revolution has brought financial stability, two new stands and a team that have come close to success with two Play-Off Final defeats at

Wembley and then the Millennium Stadium in Cardiff. Given Barry Hearn's background in the very male worlds of boxing and snooker, I'm aware that chaplaincy may have been a completely new concept for him and not too high on his list of essentials. If this is true, I admire the way he has allowed my work to continue without it appearing to sit easily with him personally. Barry Hearn has a real talent for bringing attention to something for the good of the whole, and I got caught up in one or two of these ideas in his early days. After two marriage blessings at half-times, at the second of which I allowed the bride to take a penalty, the curtain was brought down on my public role – thank goodness.

Chaplaincy is often a support role, an opportunity to get alongside players or club staff; to listen, to care, to remember and pray for. These are trusted relationships that develop. Most clubs, if asked, would recognize the need for their staff to be cared for, and chaplains can do a good job in this area if they have the skills and personality to get alongside people.

The role of the chaplain when it comes to working with the players is absolutely dependent upon the club manager. I have worked with five in the past eleven years, with each of the past three managers including our current manager having understood the role of the chaplain in very different ways. Each, I must add, has supported my involvement in the club and endeavoured to make it possible for me to work effectively with the players. Tommy Taylor took the club to two Division Three Play-Off Finals but suffered the disappointment of losing on both occasions. Tommy represented the old school in the football world. He was a tough character who said few words but meant the ones he said. He expected his players to be like him. He saw my role mainly as dealing with players who had problems. I was like the emergency services and these players were told they should see me. I did as asked, but knew these players might not risk opening up to me more fully because the manager told them they had to see me. I had become part of the hierarchy of the club, and chaplaincy works most effectively when the player feels you are on his side and not the club's.

Paul Brush is the only manager I have worked for who was a committed Christian. He sat in the unique position of wanting to produce a successful football team, while praying that players would think carefully about spiritual issues as well. He understood how to use me, to stay separate from me so players would trust me and involve me at crucial moments. Perhaps the best example of this came when he was taking the first team squad to Portugal for a pre-season training trip. Paul wanted to take me, and Barry Hearn agreed. I shared a room with two players; I ate with all the squad, trained with them, talked to them. One of the hardest barriers to break down for any chaplain is to be accepted by the group while remaining different. It is no good becoming so like them that there is no difference. For instance, getting drunk with them on a night out might make them laugh but it doesn't build credibility and trust. At all times we need to look back to what Jesus did. The Bible shows us that Jesus became one of us but was different. He lived like us, was tempted like us, got hungry like us, wept like us, but he did not sin. He remained different. As chaplains we do not become sinless beings, but we can be different. For those precious days in Portugal, barriers were being removed as the players could sense the quality of a loving God alongside them as I shared the pain of pre-season training and the joy of the pleasures of Portugal.

Martin Ling is the current manager. He expects my role as chaplain to be a positive influence on the players. It's so interesting to see the change of culture from old school football people to the new. The new are unafraid to use a number of methods instead of one. Sports psychologists are used for some people, an arm around the shoulder for another. Specific training plans are worked out for individuals rather than the one-size-fits-all approach. Much thought goes into the general well-being of a player, which has to be good. I am welcome in the club if I am good news and make the players feel at ease when I am with them. Like all the other managers I have worked for, Martin respects the need for confidentiality between the players and myself. When Jesus was around, good news was never far away. Jesus didn't depress people, he lifted them. He made people feel good about themselves because he loved them and valued them. He was interested in their lives however insignificant the people believed their lives were.

I have been struck by just how important Leyton Orient is to me. I look back to the very first time I walked on Brisbane Road and still feel it is the place in which I am more at home than any other I know. Yet this is not a one-sided relationship. The years between 1986 and 1989 are fairly unremarkable in the history of the club. There are other periods of much greater acclaim, but something remarkable happened I think. In all the fans' polls to establish their favourite players of all time, I finish first or second in front of or alongside some great names from the past. How on earth I manage to get alongside Tommy Johnston and Peter Kitchen, to name just two, is beyond me, but I am so proud that I am. God has blessed me with a role that goes beyond the players and small-office staff, to a place of ongoing influence in the lives of several thousand fans. Every football club is a unique community, held together by a common identity, history and sense of purpose. God has given to me an exalted place in the history of the club as a player, and continues to open doors for me to affect this community on a weekly basis.

The match day programme

Near the end of 2003 an opportunity arose for me to write a column for the match day programme. I was given the freedom to write whatever I wanted and see how it went. If I had known how significant an opportunity this would become I may have been too nervous to write some of those early pieces. My column has progressed and I have improved. I write about life, about people I meet, about joy and disappointment, and about football of course. I always write something that causes people to reflect on what they think and do, and sometimes about God and who he is. What an extraordinary opportunity to influence and bless this vast community. There are times when I look out at the hundred and fifty or so who come regularly to the church I am vicar of, and realize that God has also given to me a church of thousands to pastor and teach through the football club. It is something that I could never have imagined those twenty years ago when I first arrived at Brisbane Road, but it is also something that I have come to relish in the Christian faith journey. You never quite know where the journey will lead, or who you will meet up with on the way and how all of that will change you. What I do know is that I am glad to be making it.

How shall we sing the Lord's song in a strange land? That is the question the exiles in Babylon ask themselves in Psalm 137, which I quoted at the beginning of this chapter. A friend recently told me that for years he had thought of this question as one of despair. How can we ever possibly sing in a strange land? It is simply not possible. More recently he had come to wonder if this wasn't something of a rhetorical question. What ways can we find of singing the Lord's song in strange places? It is a question that challenges, and as a chaplain in the sometimes strange land of football it remains a perpetual challenge to me. Keeping the faith is one thing, but sharing it in a way that it can be properly received is quite another. For that we will need a good tune and the right words, something that Phil Mason will pick up on in the next chapter. Shall we sing a song for you? You bet!

4. By far the greatest team

PHIL MASON
Bolton Wanderers

Becoming part of the team

In recent years Bolton Wanderers have established themselves as a significant team in Premiership football. Each year they have built upon the successes of the previous season and learnt how to use their resources wisely and carefully. With limited finances they have built an impressive business and football team that prides itself in being one big family. I was privileged to join that family in 2001 as the first chaplain to the football club.

Bolton had made the decision that they wanted a club chaplain and had gone to some lengths to find the right person. This entailed looking into other places with a similar appointment and examining what the role of chaplain might include. They had also heard stories of other club chaplains and the work they had been doing through members of staff who had first-hand experience of chaplaincy from their previous clubs. It was as a result of this interest that I was invited to the club and questioned by several members of staff. Although I had been involved in chaplaincy work and knew something of sport's chaplaincy through the Commonwealth Games I really had no background in football. Indeed it was a game that I had avoided for most of my life. I was about to be taken beyond my comfort zone.

In some ways it was a shock appointment since I explained that I knew very little of the beautiful game but that I was interested in people and offering care and support for them, encouraging them to be the best they can. In the Gospel of John Jesus talks about the offer of 'life in all its fullness' and this has always been a key phrase for me.[1] So it was on this understanding that the appointment was made and an opportunity to build up a role and scope of work began.

I shall never forget going to the training ground for the very first time and meeting all the players. I have to admit I was reasonably scared, especially of facing a difficult footballing question. Being only 5ft 6ins I felt rather small and inadequate among the giants that I met, not least Big Sam himself. Names like Okotcha, Davies and Nolan meant little to me then. I realize now what great players they are, but more importantly to me what great people they are. If we are not careful we can all too easily fall into the trap of only seeing people through the filter of what they do rather than for who they really are. How many times have any of us been asked our name closely followed by the question 'And tell me, what do you do?'

Time has moved on from those early days. Now I have become a real convert to the game and of course one of the problems with converts, as we know, is that they can be more fanatical than most! So it was important that within the first six months I should get focused, and begin to get a picture and understanding of Bolton as a club, and really get alongside and know its people. This involves a great deal of 'waiting around'. As a chaplain you can often find yourself waiting simply to try to catch a chance conversation in what is a busy schedule with someone. Trying to arrange a time to talk when their diary is already overloaded, finding the right place to sit and chat can be difficult. I soon caught on to the fact that I had entered a culture in which without a mobile phone you are really not available. It is never easy trying to find the balance between spending time with the staff who work at the football ground itself and the players, the academy and the backroom staff who are based at the training ground. It proved to be a perennial problem. Where I was coming from, it was something of an alien way of life and it took some getting used to. However, I found that over the next few months I was to discover an amazing philosophy that has brought Bolton to where it is today and in which I was to find my role within that team.

Getting the best out of the team

Bolton Wanderers had held a series of away days with all the key members of staff both from the business and footballing aspects of the club. The strap line that came out of their time together was 'First Touch, Last Touch'. This principle was one that could be applied right across the work of the club. On the pitch it is clearly the first touch that makes all the difference as does the last touch of the ball before the net. On the business side of the club it is the first contact with someone that makes the difference, as is the way of customer care, until the last touch when they have left the club. For me as chaplain I could see how this principle applied to my work too. It is the first meeting, the first touch and care that I offer to supporter, member of staff or player that will make the difference. In bereavement and pastoral care the last touch takes on a whole new meaning. I had to be measured against this principle just as much as anyone else working in or being part of the team. This would inform a great deal of the work that I could do.

The club had also worked on a Purpose Statement at these away days. What was extraordinary was how full it was of 'theological' words like 'vision', 'spirit', 'love', 'inspiration', 'passion', 'caring', 'belief' and 'heart'. Here to me was the provision of further raw material for my work as I was presented with a language that I could understand and work with. All of the above had the effect of informing the club to move forward and encouraging each part of the family to get the best out of their team.

Over a number of years Sam Allardyce had been building up a 'backroom staff' to help and support his players in every way possible. Being realistic about the funds available for the purchase of players, he recognized the importance of ensuring that all the needs of his players were taken care of so that they gave their best on the pitch every time they played. Sam recognizes that a whole person comes from a balance of body, mind and spirit; the physical, emotional and spiritual. Each needs nurturing within a person to bring wholeness and to help them give their best in the way that they play. He is big on spirit.

Big Sam has a great reputation in his field as a first-class manager who can really draw out the best in people, often taking players who are either coming to the close of their playing careers or who have for one reason or another had a rough ride in other clubs. He has a great ability to see the potential in someone and then work hard with a whole team of people to draw out that potential – a 'sixth sense' as he often calls it. He brings them to Bolton and rebuilds their playing career when many might think they are no longer capable of playing in the Premiership. This sixth sense has seen him take players into the squad who are not up to full physical fitness and work with them until they are. This is true also of players who are 'unfit' in other ways too. Those who have lost their confidence in themselves and are in danger of losing their place in football are 'brought back', becoming confident players once more and often speaking about being back at the top of their game again. When I reflect upon this kind of philosophy it seems to sit so well within the context of my faith that speaks of restoration, a second chance and helping people to become all that they can be. This is the language of salvation.

As the chaplain I can play my part in helping with the fitness of players in a different way to others in the backroom team, but in a way that contributes to this holistic approach to an individual's life. Sam recognizes that even when a player is physically fit, mentally prepared and tactically on top of their game (in other words, giving their all in the top flight of football), there is still more that can be applied to get that extra 1 per cent out of them on the pitch. These extra factors can make all the difference – the difference between winning and losing. Sam and the backroom team all work very hard to put this philosophy into practice. It demands hard work, and means a multidisciplinary approach and team understanding of how each person contributes to the whole. The chaplain, working closely with the sports psychologists within the club, plays a vital role in this partnership.

Part of my role as chaplain is about getting alongside the players and getting to know them; not to interfere, but to make sure they know I am available. Simply being around is all part of this role. It is not glamorous and not about being in the limelight, but simply about being there. There is something very profound to me about that aspect of any ministry when it is about 'being' rather than always 'doing'. It takes time to build up trust and relationships but it pays off in the end. The important thing in chaplaincy is that people recognize you are there for them and their agenda and not the other way round.

One of the key elements to Jesus' ministry was what I would describe as the 'ministry of interruption'. Often within the gospel passages we encounter Jesus travelling in one direction with one purpose in mind and find him giving attention to others in a completely different direction and set of circumstances. For example, the healing of Jairus's daughter in which he is interrupted by the woman who had been haemorrhaging for many years.[2] Another example might be where he ends up at Zacchaeus's house for tea,[3] or how he ends up feeding the five thousand.[4] This ministry of interruption is often how it works for me in the football club. I may go expecting to talk to certain people and end up doing a whole host of other tasks, speaking to those I had never imagined seeing that day; becoming a part of their agenda rather than them being on mine!

All faiths and none

A further dimension to the make-up of the team in Bolton is the incredible mix of nationalities and cultures. It truly is an international squad of players, made up of over sixteen nationalities. To bring such a diversity of people together to make up a team and build up the philosophy that I have described above takes real hard work and commitment. You either see such diversity as a hindrance to what you are trying to achieve or recognize that diversity as a gift. Sam clearly sees it as a gift and makes maximum use of it while ensuring that care and support is offered to help both players and their families settle down and feel part of life in this country and within Bolton. This gives me the opportunity to work very closely with the two player liaison officers that look after the practical needs both of the players and of their families.

I have already outlined how a series of away days resulted in shaping up a strap line and purpose statement, and these kinds of away days play a vital role in the club's life. Taking a multidisciplined approach, and under the direction of Mike Forde the club's performance consultant, the first team away days spend time reflecting on what has happened over the past months. Time is spent planning for the future, setting realistic goals and targets and looking to ways to develop the work that will improve the club and its position.

At one of these days we spent some time looking at the multi-cultural and multifaith mix of the squad that followed from some simple research that Dr Mark Nesti (counselling sports psychologist to the club) and I had carried out with the players.

We discovered an amazing mix of religious belief and faith within the squad – a far higher percentage than I first imagined and in stark contrast to the residue of 'faith' within our culture in wider society. Represented on this day were those of the Christian faith (including many different denominations), Muslim, Jew and Rastafarian. Their understanding of faith was well developed as was the importance of that faith to them. Many of the players have come from countries where faith is very much part of the fabric of society. When asked questions about how important their faith was to them out of a score of ten, over half of the squad came up with a score of ten. Three-quarters of the remaining members scored between four and six, with the rest showing no score.

From this work we recognized the importance of learning more about each of the religions and faiths represented and we were able to draw together a calendar of important festivals and holy days so that we could acknowledge and celebrate them appropriately. We also recognized the need to create the right kind of space for quiet reflection or prayer and meditation so that individual players could make use of it as would be most helpful to them in their spirituality.

Through the research we also discovered other important factors that have an impact upon a person. We have described them as 'faith drivers'. These are aspects within a person of faith that add to their motivation for what they do. That is not to say that some if not all of these drivers are not found in people with no faith, but it seems that they are more likely to be found in people with faith.

The first of these is a sense of life with a purpose. However God is defined, there is a real sense that because of the existence of a Being that has a plan and direction for the world then an individual with faith feels that they too are contributing in some way to the whole and have a purpose for life. They may not fully understand what that purpose is, and might still be searching for it, but there still is a sense of purpose.

Second, there is a motivation other than simply the self. In sport, self-motivation is vital but what I mean here is that there is a recognition that this is not just about self, but rather about others. There is often a greater awareness of others and a wider sense of responsibility towards others, and this clearly helps in the context of any team sport and especially in the context of Premiership football.

Third, there is often a better understanding of success and failure. How we understand success is very important, and also how we measure that success. The danger is that it is often simply measured in material gain, better contracts and lifestyles, and there is a great deal of pressure in the modern game to conform to such an approach to life. Faith can help bring a balanced understanding of success and recognize that failure can often be turned into opportunity and success. Our club psychologist works with these ideas in promoting a more existential-phenomenological psychology which recognizes the balance of body, mind and spirit and the place of anxiety, courage, meaning, identity and authenticity. It avoids the trap of suggesting life is great all the time and all we have to do is think positive and all will be well. It recognizes the reality of life with its ups and downs and is realistic about how to handle those feelings.

In looking at issues of success and failure I often quote the picture of Jesus. He was born in poverty and lived for only about thirty-three years. He spent most of his life in obscurity, never wrote a book, never had any public position. His followers, the team of twelve, deserted him; he was crucified as a common criminal with two thieves, and yet over two thousand years later millions of people are still following him. Is that a picture of success or failure, or is it both? Such a question often opens a great debate with players and academy lads alike.

I hope that you can glean from the above the important stress that the club makes upon the recognition of 'spirit' and indeed the power of the human spirit that goes beyond the mental and physical resources within a person.

Here is a club that takes seriously the role of the chaplain and wants to integrate that work into its understanding and philosophy. This is not only the case on the playing side of the staff team but also in the context of the wider life of the club and working with both the staff at the Reebok Stadium and the supporters.

Rules of play

The chief executive of Bolton Wanderers, Allan Duckworth, has taken a particular interest in the developing work of the chaplain and has been keen to integrate the role into the wider work of the club. Working with him and Margaret O'Brien, the personnel training and development manager, we drew together a job description for the chaplain that clearly defined the scope of work that I would be involved in and looked at development opportunities for the work. This then gave the club a measure by which to assess the effectiveness (or not) of the chaplain. It seemed to me to be vital that I could be measured for my work just as much as any other member of the club staff.

Margaret O'Brien has been leading the club's work in meeting the standard for Investors in People. I was very keen for the club to pursue this standard and my own church is the only Methodist church in the county, and the second church in the whole of the country, to have gained this standard. Clearly what is important here is not so much the gaining of the standard but rather putting the principles in place so that you really are 'Investing in People'.

Following the success of gaining this standard within the club, Margaret has been putting together a package that outlines the benefits of working at Bolton Wanderers, particularly concentrating on the additional support that those employed by the club can expect. In among that list is the work of the club chaplain; the one-to-one support that can be offered and the opportunity for ongoing counselling support through the

Simeon Centre Counselling service that operates as a partnership project from my own church in Bolton.

Here we can see again that holistic approach being drawn out in the philosophy and work ethos of the club. Working closely with Margaret has given me the opportunity to identify particular staff needs and offer support at some of their significant life moments, including bereavement and breakdown of relationships, as well as anniversaries, birthdays and the birth of a child. All of this work gives an added dimension to the care and support that can be offered to the staff across all departments and helps create the family club that Bolton has such a great reputation for being.

This more strategic approach to the work has been taken forward in other ways to include the shaping up of additional policies for the club so that we have a clear understanding of what to do under different circumstances. We live in a culture that has in recent years become more and more secularized. The traditional route of institutional religion is very much on the decline. The traditional church has lost significant ground. Yet in spite of this background there is an increasing awareness of spirituality. This has often been described as a kind of pick-and-mix approach where people choose the bits that they like from various religious traditions to create a spirituality that seems right for them. In the course of this process people have been expressing their spirituality and raw human emotions in a whole variety of new ways. Wherever you go now you see roadside shrines appearing where people have placed flowers or lit candles, left significant verses or poems, all in memory of a loved one who has died in tragic circumstances. This is the new vehicle to express loss that has replaced the church that once was at the heart of the community.

In the context of the football club you find that this kind of expression of spirituality has grown too. For many people their football is a way of life and, as other chapters in this book describe, their club means everything to them. The football club is their church through which they express their religion. The match day plays out a whole liturgy of its own, drawing people together through fellowship, the sense of belonging and team spirit. There is a sense of being there for a common purpose and a lot of this expresses itself through the singing, chanting and arm waving.

It is no surprise therefore that people want to express legitimately their sense of loss and grief through the club in some way. We have increasingly found, as in other clubs, people wanting to place flowers somewhere at the club, and often they have been tied to the nearest flagpole. People have requested the scattering of their loved one's ashes on the pitch. At times, when a former player or a supporter has died in tragic circumstances there has been a cry from the fans for a minute's silence before a match, or for the flags at the front entrance of the club to be lowered to half mast.

With all this background in mind, we set about writing a Bereavement Policy for the club. This work was again carried out with a multidisciplinary approach in mind, drawing together people from different areas of the club, including a board director and the club secretary. The policy looks in detail at how we as a club should respond in different circumstances following the death of anyone attached to the club. The emphasis is always on the support of the family and their loss and how we can help and support that family in this period. We have also written into the policy any actions that we might take following the death of someone who might be high profile at the club, recognizing the need to respond quickly and appropriately, allowing family and supporters to express their grief and sorrow. In the world of 24-hour media attention we recognized the need to be prepared and ready for all possibilities so that we can respond with the proper dignity and respect for the people involved.

Following on from the development of this policy we have looked at drawing together a number of services that are available for anyone associated with the club. We offer the opportunity for the scattering of ashes on the pitch with a short memorial service. We now have a Book of Remembrance where people can put in the names of their loved ones on the appropriate page. Each anniversary the page will be opened to reveal the names of those who died on that particular day. We have placed this book in a case at the front entrance of the club to give 24-hour, 7-days a week access to ensure people can come when they want. This space has a permanent memorial and receptacles for people to place flowers, being far more satisfactory than simply taping them to a flagpole. We have also developed our 'Walk Way of Fame' where people can purchase memorial bricks that are placed near the entrance of the club.

For the past two years we have held a service of remembrance and thanksgiving at the close of the season where we read out the names of all those within the Book of Remembrance or on the memorial bricks. Loved ones gather and have the opportunity to light a candle in memory of the one they have come to remember before we go to the pitch side for a time of silence and a blessing. The numbers attending have already doubled to over two hundred people, perhaps illustrating the need for such a space and for being church in a different and more accessible way.

One of the club's resources

It was Big Sam who said to me on one occasion, 'Phil, you are one of the club's resources.' I don't think you can get better than that. In that statement there is recognition of the role and part the chaplain can play. Here is an understanding that I am simply one of hundreds of other resources and that my agenda should be the club's and not my own.

In my relatively short time at the club, and indeed my 'baptism of fire' introduction to the world of football, I have discovered that it is important for people who are part of the club to understand why you are there and what your role is. A clear definition and purpose has helped integrate my work into the fabric of the club and for the club to take that role seriously.

Traditionally the town of Bolton was part of the cotton industry; a spinning town more than a weaving town. That industry has now long gone. In Bolton we believe there is a new fabric to be weaved, one of a multicultural society. The football club is in the business of weaving together many threads coming from a whole variety of countries and cultures to create a successful and winning team. I feel privileged to play my small part as the chaplain to that club and in a background kind of way to assist in the weaving of that fabric.

5. No one likes us?

OWEN BEAMENT
Millwall

Dr Mervyn Stockwood, the larger-than-life former Bishop of Southwark (and larger than most of his contemporaries put together), always believed that humour and laughter were an intrinsic part of the gospel. 'Owen,' he said, 'I am delighted that you have a chance to teach at a local school, but you would do better to teach sports rather than religion; you know far more about that!'

So in September 1966 I donned my old Saracens rugby shirt – which impressed nobody – and set off for John Evelyn School. There I collected an enthusiastic bunch of children and headed off for Deptford Park, where for an hour and a half the newly formed GLC had allocated the two gravel football pitches to the school.

On arrival, a look of dismay came over us all as a large group of adults were playing football on both pitches. 'They should be at work,' I mumbled, 'not playing about at this time of day.' 'They are at work, Sir', came the reply. 'That's Millwall.'

Before I had thought what we should do, a man came over to me and asked, 'Are you supposed to have these pitches?' I was pleased that my mind moved rather fast on that occasion, correctly guessing that he might be the manager. I replied, 'Yes, but if you can manage with one for the moment, I'll manage with the boys on the other.' He was very grateful, and we continued to train on adjacent pitches. I suppose that there are not many priests who have been able to provide their local team with training facilities. All through my ministry I have found myself in unusual situations, as though God was saying, 'There you are, see what you can do with that.' Sadly, I realize looking back that I have wasted many of those opportunities. I am glad I did not waste this one.

My reward for giving the training ground to Millwall was an invitation to the ground for a match, and so began a lasting bond of friendship and my part conversion from rugby to football – although in matters of sport (as well as religion) I have always felt a great sympathy for those of other persuasions.

My first visit to The Den hooked me and opened the way for some special friendship. I am forever grateful to Bill Nelan, a club director at that time, who befriended me and introduced me to what is now my favourite pastime and another 'Religion'. He was the first to take me on a golf course and as my enthusiasm grew – far faster than my skill – it opened up many friendships. Those were very relaxed days, and after training the players would often meet in the Royal Archer for lunch – rolls and beer, it was before the days of pasta and fruit – and then adjourn to Shooters Hill Golf Club.

Under those circumstances it was not hard just to take the kindness and generosity offered. I was pleased to realize that some people liked to have me there to make use of me because I was a priest. One of the most important bits of advice a priest can be given came to me from the secretary of our church boxing club when he said, 'Put yourself about.' If we are out and about God can use us; if we stay in church we shall become introverted religious nuts. From those early days people often came to me with some simple but searching questions, especially, 'Will I see my loved ones again?'

I remember at this time that a friend, whom I had known for several years, gasped in amazement at any involvement with Millwall. He once visited The Den to support Crystal Palace and thought he was lucky to escape alive. 'I don't wonder that no one likes you,' he said.

I would like to think that I became involved with Millwall because I decided to follow the example of Christ, who always seemed to back the underdog and support lepers, prostitutes and outcasts. I cannot claim any holy and pious motives. I simply grew very fond of the Deptford and Bermondsey environment because deep down the people are wonderful – loyal, no pretence, 'what you see is what you get', and great humour.

However, I soon realized why Millwall had developed their reputation. It is a reputation that is certainly not deserved, but on the other hand one that the fans rather like. It gives a distinct character and hopefully puts fear into opponents.

As far back as I can remember Millwall was referred to as 'the Team in the heart of London's Dockland'. It was still in the days when the docks were active. The Surrey Docks Canal ran very close to the ground in the days when it was the largest timber dock in Europe, and a majority of the home crowd were dockers. The approach to the ground through the Victorian railway arches of Cold Blow Lane would have frightened most visitors; the noise from the crowd was multi-decibel, the spectators were only a few feet from the pitch and the language was expressive if not Shakespearean.

But the community around The Den was very close-knit; 'look after your own' was often heard. Even today people lament the passing of the days when front doors could be left open. This sense of being a separate community was passed on to Millwall and has remained. The word 'Millwall' has become a synonym for violence, but out of journalistic jargon rather than a sense of justice.

It does not help much when the club is patronized, and comments on the wonderful work of the community scheme are accompanied by such phrases as 'trying to live down its violent history'. On 19 August 2003 *The Times* published an article entitled 'Hi-tech hooligans lure youths to football "firms" '. The table itemizing arrests and acts of violent disorder found that Fulham, Charlton, Gillingham and Wimbledon (in the top two divisions) were the only clubs who had fewer arrests and evictions for unacceptable behaviour.

I can fully understand why Christ so often took the side of the less privileged and sometimes despised sections of society, and it is not only out of a sense of justice. Very often they are people with very genuine values and simply good, relaxing company.

Millwall supporters may not be religious in the established sense (although if there is a midday kick-off at the New Den on a Sunday the church empties much faster after Mass than usual!). Nevertheless there have been many occasions when the church has been appreciated. Two of the most moving times were following the Hillsborough and Bradford disasters. On both occasions the church was full – players, staff, directors and hundreds of fans – all wishing to say their prayers and remember others in the world of football who had experienced much suffering. On both occasions a very generous collection was passed on to the disaster fund.

Neither can I think of any time when anyone has been anything other than friendly and respectful of the fact that I always wear a black suit and clerical collar. On one occasion, while driving into the ground on a match day, a small boy looked at me and asked his Dad, 'Who's that?' I was driving slowly enough to hear what seemed to be a proud reply: 'In this club we even have our own pie and liquor.'

After one match I was chatting to the chairman of a visiting club. I deduced from our conversation that he was either a regular worshipper or at least very sympathetic to the Church. He let slip that he was pleased to see me dressed as a priest, and lamented the fact that his own club chaplain seemed shy about wearing clerical dress. 'Perhaps he is frightened of what people think,' he added. Nevertheless, I do respect that not all clergy like the black suit and clerical collar approach.

Any warmth and kindness is not reserved for me alone. Christmas is a busy time, but I have on one or two occasions placed the choir at the entrance of the gates and sung carols. Very few people walk past without throwing something into our buckets, and all comments are favourable.

The reason for collecting at Christmas is to finance a large all-day party on Christmas Day itself, and singing carols can become a licence to print money. This was never more true than a few years ago in a pub in Meopham. I had played in a pre-Christmas 'Turkey-Trot' golf society meeting, and was chatting about Christmas when the landlord overheard me. 'Bring your kids down our way,' he suggested. He arranged for us to visit three other pubs and finish at his. After a few carols in the bar he invited us to try the restaurant. I must now explain that the choir wear blue and white robes and at Christmas they also wear a Millwall scarf. No sooner had we finished the first verse of 'Away in a manger' than someone shouted, 'Sing us the Millwall song!' As soon as we had completed (out of respect for our Lord) the words 'And fit us for heaven to live with thee there' we launched into 'It's Saturday in Cold Blow Lane' (at Millwall we have our own song, not one adopted from someone else's collection!). At that point, amid cheers, it seemed that everyone in the restaurant was making ten and twenty pound notes into darts and flying them towards us! I realized that the particular part of Kent we were in is very much Millwall and South East London exodus country. They may have moved away from The Den, but they still had blue and white blood.

That sense of belonging is something I have come to treasure over the years, and has led me to feel a deep desire for justice. Again I cannot claim that it is a calculated opinion based on my reading of the gospel, but just a natural feeling for a club that is at the heart of this community. My first public expression was during the mid-1960s when, allegedly, the referee was attacked after a game. I wrote to *The Times* – and I am not in any way an enthusiastic writer of letters to papers – to explain the other side. I wrote about all the good things that the club was doing and the contribution that the players made in the day-to-day events of the community. In those days there was a football league magazine that repeated my letter, but I do not think it swayed too much public opinion. 'Millwall' as a synonym for 'undesirable' was too useful.

It was around 1990 that everything was suddenly made official. A new manager had come to the club, and he had a good experience of chaplaincy in a previous position. The club secretary phoned me to ask if I might be interested, but I was away on holiday at the time. When I returned there was a letter waiting for me just saying, 'We have appointed you.' Of course they knew I would be flattered, and I can honestly say that it is the only position with regard to my priesthood that I might ever have sought. Soon after my appointment I was sent a short quotation, on a postcard, attributed to Archbishop Trench who lived from 1807 to 1886. I still have it in my sacristy and it reads, 'Thou camest not to this place by accident, it is the very place God meant for thee.' The idea of letting God set the agenda has become very appealing over the years, and looking back

I have seen the point of leaving to him far more than we often do. Church committees and synods (for which I do not have great enthusiasm) come up with some wonderful ideas, but so often in retrospect it is not what God intended. I remember the words of Christ to Peter, 'You are thinking in man's ways not God's ways.'

So there I am, still at the Old Den, and now officially chaplain. I spent a while with the manager, who took me to the changing room to introduce me to the players – some of whom I knew already. I remember saying to myself then, 'What on earth do I do now?' I decided, after due thought, just to watch the football. We drew 1–1 with West Ham.

Gradually people became aware that I was the chaplain, and never have I received anything but kindness and courtesy, always laced with considerable humour. It must be the same for every chaplain that the repeated chuckle when we lose is 'You were obviously not praying hard enough'. That was said after we appeared on 22 May 2004 at Cardiff in the FA Cup Final. My reply was, 'I got you to Cardiff; you do the rest!'

Of course we all know that simply praying for a team to win is not on. (Mind you, in the FA Cup semi-final at Old Trafford, when we were hanging on by a single goal, I did wonder if I might give the Lord a nudge!) However, praying for the club, for the players and for the staff is the basis of it all. Every Saturday at All Saints we pray for Millwall at the morning Mass. Every time I visit the ground or the training ground I say a short prayer asking that if I can be of use I should be steered in the right direction. I believe it has landed me in some very interesting and worthwhile situations, not least at times of bereavement and sickness.

I soon learned that the ministry of any chaplain is varied and covers all aspects of the club and a variety of people. 'Do not be overawed by the great nor ignore the insignificant.' In the eyes of God all are equal, be they an international star or a junior fan.

The largest, and probably most enduring, part of any club is the fans, still many of whom can remember the 1930s. I have a friend who is willing to quote the entire team from the 1937 FA Cup semi-final, when we were beaten by Sunderland. (How history nearly repeats itself! In 2004 we beat Sunderland to reach the final.) Many fans are aware that the club has a chaplain and make use of me, especially as I have the privilege of appearing in the match day magazine in the who's who. Frequently this results in me being invited to take funerals. The most important thing I carry in my funeral bag is the CD of the Millwall song, and many times we finish with the song that means so much to fans, and, we believe, is something that unites us with those beyond this world.

However, Millwall is more that that – it is a common bond. I vividly remember the time when I was asked to take a funeral service for an elderly man who had three sons. They were all very devoted to Millwall and had their own executive box but had not realized that I was the chaplain to the club. I arranged to visit them, and was politely shown into the front parlour and offered a cup of tea – from a cup and saucer, which at once separated me from everyone else – and was left with Mum to get on with whatever they expected me to do. After a while one of them kindly came in to enquire whether or not I had a car and was it parked safely. I said that I thought it would be safe as it had my Millwall stickers in the window, and I thought that meant the locals would respect it. There was a pause, during which he came to terms with a priest using the word 'Millwall', and once he had established that I was genuine let out a few expletives in amazement and called in his brothers. After that, Mum and their deceased father played very little part in the conversation. Most of the time was spent in discussing the fortunes and misfortunes of the club. From then on, I was a welcome guest in their box, and shared a few G & Ts.

I was asked recently what the Church was doing being represented in Millwall, because it seemed to the questioner that the world of the Church and the world of Millwall were far apart. Alas, that may seem true to many, but it can never be said of the story of the gospel. I love to remind people that Jesus was a carpenter – a member of the working classes, not even a vicar!

Many times after a funeral, when I am enjoying people's company at the reception, Millwall crops up in conversation and it is more than just a chat about football. It reflects, albeit by inference, that the Church is properly part of every aspect of life.

One equally important part of life and ministry as a chaplain is weddings. Contrary to much popular belief, one cannot just get married anywhere; the regulations are about having a marriage recognized in the eyes of the law, not so much in the eyes of God. I believe we can lay claim at Millwall to performing the first ever wedding on a football pitch. It was so different that ITV told the story throughout the country. The couple were both very devoted to Millwall and asked if they could be married at the club and on the pitch. First of all they came to church for their marriage to be recognized as legal in a small but regular ceremony. The next day they invited all their friends to celebrate their wedding in what was virtually a repeat ceremony, but without any registers, on the pitch itself. But the unusual did not stop there. The bridegroom appeared for his wedding in Millwall away kit and the bride and bridesmaids came in the blue of Millwall's home kit. Apart from that, the couple exchanged their vows as normal but in front of their family and friends, and we prayed and joined in singing Christmas carols (it was the second half of December). Finally the couple walked out of camera, off the pitch and into the changing room to live happily ever after while our choir sang 'Away in a manger'.

That was the first, and most unusual, wedding, but by no means the last. We have celebrated wedding vows and blessings for several couples, staff and fans alike, and we do so on a very important principle. If we believe that God can come to a cow shed at the back of a pub in Bethlehem, then nowhere is beyond his reach.

To the outsider, such weddings may seem just a gimmick, but if that were the case I should not be involved. Millwall is very dear to people, as are many clubs. God is also very much at the heart of the lives of many people and the combination of the two is totally natural.

The smallest and most transient part of any club, but the best-known part, is the players, and Millwall is no exception. Nevertheless, they are the part that is most on show, and when people name a club they think primarily of the team: 'Millwall are doing well' means that the team are winning; 'Millwall are doing badly' means that the team are not doing well. The success or otherwise of the first team affects the club and far beyond. When Millwall reached the Cup Final in 2004 the entire community of South East London seemed to turn out for the parade through Bermondsey and Lewisham to share in the achievement. The credit for getting there was down to just a few players, often referred to as the gladiators of the modern Circus Maximus!

Many well-known players are forever in the spotlight, and earn more in a week than most people in this country earn in two years; but few are in that category. Most professional players may earn more than the average person, but a career may not be very long for many of them. Nevertheless, while they are in the limelight they are local heroes; youngsters will seek their autographs and they will appear frequently in the local press.

I was talking recently with a young chauffeur after a funeral while waiting for the mourners to look at their flowers and chat to one another. The conversation soon came round to Millwall and he asked, 'Do you actually talk to the players?' I realized that to him, and I suppose to many others, they are as distant and exalted as Hollywood film stars. And yet they are, of course, ordinary human beings like the rest of us. Like the rest of us they often need someone with whom to talk.

I recall instances when players have been injured; they have been grateful for someone to see them in hospital, not that humour is ever far away. Some years ago one of our players broke his leg in a tackle. Shortly after the accident I traced him to a local hospital, but just as I arrived I found that he was about to be taken into the operating theatre. The surgeon was most courteous and said he would wait for a moment while I chatted with him. He took one look at me and exclaimed, 'Oh no, I'm not that bad am I?'

Sometimes hospital visits are an opportunity to meet players' families, and players, like anyone else, depend on their families for their security. It has been a privilege to talk with mums and dads of young players, and it may be surprising to know that many are quite keen to share their allegiance to the Church with me, and pleased to know that football clubs are not totally godless territory.

I recall a visit to the training ground when an injured player greeted me with the words, 'Are you still praying for me?' On another occasion a player called me over and sat me down opposite him and then said, 'I'm a Christian.' And so the conversation developed. Or again a player who was seriously ill revealed to me the whole story of his illness and successful recovery. Such moments are what it is all about.

Players can exercise considerable influence on young people, and often it is for the good.

A few years ago I took a funeral service for a young woman who very sadly had died in her thirties. She had a young daughter who was very enthusiastic about her support for Millwall. I was discussing this event with the manager after a pre-season training session when he made a very kind suggestion. 'Why don't you bring her to a game, but beforehand bring her to the changing room and I'll get the lads to cheer her up a bit and show her we care?' The game in question turned out to be a pre-season friendly with Liverpool, so some forty-five minutes before the kick-off I took her and a friend with her dad to the changing rooms. All the players knew what had happened and without exception they were marvellous. Dad was taking photos as fast as he could.

The manager then suggested that I have a word with Roy Evans who was the Liverpool manager at the time to ask if he would mind if I took the little party to meet their players. I asked and he was only too delighted to oblige. 'Give me two minutes to explain what it is all about,' he said, 'and then bring them over.'

Accordingly I took them to meet the Liverpool players, and again they were marvellous. By now the girls' eyes were popping out of their heads, being in the presence of international stars, but the best was yet to come. I hope he will excuse me for mentioning him by name, but it was an act of real kindness. In the corner of the changing room was John Barnes, who at that time was a well-known international. Seeing the girl's father with the camera he called to the girls and beckoned them over. Overwhelmed, and slightly nervous – of course they knew who he was – they walked over to him. He said to them, 'Is there any chance of me having my photo with you, please?' I believe that act of kindness continues to have a very deep effect on the girl in question.

A player's time in front of the crowds is short, and soon after he has gone the memory fades. For some, the legend will never go. One such player was Harry Cripps. He was such a favourite, always gave 110 per cent and had the appearance of being related to a centurion tank. Yet off the field a more delightful and courteous gentleman would be hard to find. His time in the 1960s and '70s was a good period for Millwall, and I remember well a Cup match against Tottenham when the crowd at the Old Den numbered forty-five thousand. Last season one of the members of that team was at the New Den and introduced himself to me. When I told him I remembered him he was both surprised and delighted; he seemed to think he had been relegated to the archives.

Players can and do bring a great sense of occasion to events, especially where young footballers are involved. The presentation night at the Oxford and Bermondsey club has been made very special, not just because some of the players come to give away the awards, but because they stay behind for a chat and a photo. There are pictures on the walls of the club going back many years.

I suppose that if there is one special jewel in the Millwall family it is the community scheme. Gradually building up over the years it now touches the lives of so many youngsters. Cynics have said that Millwall had such a bad image that they had to do something, but it is far more than a publicity exercise. There are some very desolate estates near the club and coaches from the scheme go to all places to give the young people something to occupy their time, to keep them from idleness and to give them an interest.

If there is a charity event in the community the club will do all it can to support it. Ground collections are abundant for worthwhile local charities. I was very privileged to play for Millwall, not football but in a golf team representing the club at the Mayor of Lewisham's charity golf day in aid of breast cancer research.

Every year, and with the help of the Deptford Rotary Club, we have a special day out at the Lingfield races for elderly people from the area, and again the staff of the club make a great contribution by helping. Sadly, two years ago I failed to heed their advice. There was a horse running called Forever My Lord. Almost everyone else backed it – I was not so tempted. It was first past the post, and at 15–1!

Much of the work of a chaplain is very personal, and strictly confidential. There are times when players and other members of the staff wish to talk with someone from the club but not employed by the club and answerable to a higher authority than even the chairman. Such occasions are always a privilege. But there is much more to it than that. Above all it involves just being about and being available – and most of all having the ability to laugh.

I believe and hope that I have a genuine and deep affection for the club, and count it as a privilege to be involved. I felt it more than ever when I was invited to join players and staff in celebrating our appearance at the club dinner after the 2004 Cup Final. It was a great evening, and a privilege to be there.

I always like to assure people that despite the projected image, for all the times that people chant 'No one likes us – we don't care', for all the memories of the old dockland, Millwall is just like Wagner's music – not as bad as it sounds.

6. With hope in your heart

BILL BYGROVES
Liverpool

A ministry of reconciliation

*On Merseyside the locals have a passionate sense of community
and it is a passion that spills over into the life of its football
teams. Church leaders in Liverpool have long recognized this
and most notably the late Derek Worlock and David Sheppard,
as bishops to the Roman Catholic and Anglican communities,
made a point of it with their attendance at Anfield and Goodison. But while they recognized the intense rivalry between the
footballing communities on derby day, they made their point
in emphasizing the need for communities to live alongside and
get along with each other. At each match one bishop would
wear the red and white of Liverpool and the other the blue and
white of Everton, and at half-time they would swap scarves. It
was always a nice touch, but it made a serious if symbolic point
to any who cared to watch. Bill Bygroves is perhaps unique
among chaplains in that although he might not be able to claim,
like Owen Beament, that he arranged pitches in the local park
for the first-team squad to train on, he has been, among other
things, in his long association with Liverpool FC, a youth and
community coach. He is now the club chaplain and has been
for some years.*

Like many clubs, Liverpool takes its responsibility in the local
community very seriously, but we all know that football has
been a global game for decades and for many top-flight clubs in
the United Kingdom there have been a number of sorties into
the glamorous world of European competition. Liverpool Foot-

ball Club has been among the most successful in recent decades, winning the European Cup on five occasions. But it is a club that has had to face tragedy too. It has had to take its sense of local community responsibility onto a wider stage, and on this stage, under the public eye and the scrutiny of a sometimes merciless press, it has had to grow a ministry of reconciliation. Bill has been involved in that ministry and in this chapter takes up the story and tells of its importance for the club he serves.

The day of 29 May 1985 was something of a dark day for European football and for Liverpool Football Club in particular. The European Cup Final, instead of being an occasion of celebration, turned into an occasion of shame, pain and death. Thirty-nine Juventus fans lost their lives in what football history now records as the Heysel Stadium disaster. Entire families were torn apart by grief as many experienced the loss of a child or a parent. It was a painful night and one that left many memories scarred with the void of human loss. In addition, the reputation of two great European football clubs was stained by the violence that was perpetrated that same night. There has been a lot of ink spilled over the causes and who might have been responsible – about the safety arrangements, ticketing and policing – and I have no real wish to dwell on any of that here, for what I experienced in the weeks and months and years that followed was something that hasn't made the news headlines, which some might think is equally shameful. How do two communities ever recover from something like that? For many at the football club, it was the ongoing challenge of being involved in some sort of reconciliation ministry.

Tuesday 5 April 2005 was the first time since that disaster that Liverpool and Juventus had played against each other. This was the European Champions League Cup and here were the same two great clubs, drawn together on the biggest stage in football, playing for a place in the semi-final of Europe's most prestigious competition. Everyone could look forward to a feast of footballing excellence with brilliant technique, fierce competitiveness, tactical astuteness and individual flair, with each team totally committed to winning the game.

As a game the event lived up to its billing and the teams to their reputations and traditions in European competition. Over the two legs of this part of the competition we were treated to two marvellous games, the outcome being that Liverpool overcame Juventus on the field of play to claim a place in the semifinal of the trophy they would go on to win. There was great pride in all of that and rightly so. However, for me it wasn't for the football that this game was to be remembered; it was the friendship recovered after twenty years and the sense of reconciliation between the two clubs both on and off the field that marked this game as unique.

As chaplain of Liverpool Football Club it was my privilege to be asked to be part of a team of people who would be involved in what was to become a considerable peacemaking and bridge-building process. It was a process that had been started 20 years before, but in 2005 both communities decided that it should be marked with an official service of reconciliation between cities and clubs and remembrance of those who had died.

The bereaved Italian families were led by Mr Otto Lorrentini who acted as their spokesman. He had been asked if there was any place in their hearts for forgiveness over Heysel. It was an important question since the whole business of forgiveness can often be glossed over in a rather glib fashion. He helped us see that forgiveness never walks alone and that it always goes hand in hand with the expression of sorrow and regret. For those families who had suffered the loss through death and injury, the pain and deep hurt was still fresh and for some still raw. While feelings of remorse and sadness might have abounded, there had been little public expression, and yet the families wanted to mark the twentieth year of the Heysel disaster as a possible turning point for themselves and the clubs. We needed to do something about this.

Responding to Mr Lorrentini, Mr Rick Parry, Chief Executive of Liverpool Football Club began a process which was to culminate in a friendly match between the under 19s of Liverpool and Juventus, which turned out to have a wonderful sense of friendship, providing everyone with a platform upon which to build real reconciliation and ongoing respect for the two clubs. Importantly it also gave some closure, and all of this took place in recognition of Mr Lorrentini's work.

Jesus said, 'Blessed are the peacemakers', which has always been an inspiration to those seeking a ministry of reconciliation. Peacemaking and reconciliation are never easy when we try to live them out, but they are an integral part of living out the Christian faith in the world. We looked for opportunities to do this during those weeks of meeting with club officials at Juventus and during the events surrounding the quarter-final of the Champions League match of 2005. I felt an increasing sense of responsibility for the task and one that was a privilege for the club chaplain to undertake.

During the period of time around the home match between Liverpool and Juventus, Mr Parry sanctioned a number of initiatives that tried to foster a real emphasis on Christian forgiveness and reconciliation. The first of these was the publication of a formal apology. A local Liverpool newspaper ran a headline which read 'SORRY'; the article that accompanied it expressed the sadness and sorrow of the people of the city of Liverpool and of Liverpool Football Club and its supporters. This was accompanied by the publication of a personal apology from one of the fans who had been involved in the Heysel disaster.

The naming of the game between Liverpool and Juventus as 'THE FRIENDSHIP GAME' was the next initiative and it was delivered with a good deal of personal interaction. Juventus supporters were personally welcomed at the Liverpool airport upon their arrival in what was the start of a very warm and genuine welcome to the city and the club. The game itself saw the publication of a special match programme containing a history of reconciliation work that had been ongoing between the clubs in the last twenty years; this initiative also saw the production of a special friendship scarf with 'You'll never walk alone' and 'In memory and friendship' printed in Italian and English bearing the colours of Liverpool and Juventus. These were simple touches but were very well received by those who participated in the event. The supporters took part in a friendly game of football before the match itself, played at the Liverpool Youth Academy. The participants played in the spirit of good humour and fun. This was much publicized and set the mood for the competitive match itself, at which a special banner, bearing the names of those who had died at Heysel, was paraded onto the Anfield pitch carried by Liverpool fans and received by Juventus fans. This banner was symbolically handed over by the two former club captains, both of whom had been involved on that fateful night – English international Phil Neal and Juventus captain Michel Platini. After this symbolic presentation, the Liverpool supporters stood in silence as a gesture of respect, memory and friendship.

In the return fixture at Turin, the mood continued with a special service of remembrance attended by the chairman and chief executive of Liverpool Football Club and the president and dignitaries of Juventus, along with former players and current club captains. Here they presented flowers and a plaque in memory of the dead and in friendship to Mr Lorrentini. During the game both teams wore specially produced bands with 'friendship' printed in Italian and English on them. These bands subsequently became available for the fans to wear.

All of this was followed up six months after the quarter-final tie with a special visit of the chief executives and the under-19s teams of both Liverpool and Juventus to the city of Arriza. At the invitation of Mr Lorrentini, both sets of officials and players first attended a civic dinner, in which gifts were exchanged and speeches of friendship were made. Liverpool Football Club also presented the Mayor of Arriza with a gift that became known as 'the Lorrentini Friendship Cup'. It became a trophy for the young people of Arriza to compete for. Mr Parry expressed how humbled and privileged he and the club felt to be involved in this gesture of friendship and reconciliation. The following day, in the beautiful cathedral of Arriza, I was asked as the chaplain of the football club to bring the greetings and the condolences of the City of Liverpool and of the directors, staff and players of the club. I was also able to deliver a message of hope based on the club's anthem of 'You'll Never Walk Alone'. This message was well received by the families, officials and players alike and it felt as though a real healing had begun. In what had started as shadowy darkness, it felt that the light of Christ was beginning to shine through. After the service a friendly game of football took place. Many of the children of Arriza came to watch. Liverpool lost the game by two goals to one but everyone agreed that we had won so many friends as a result of our search for reconciliation.

A poem called 'The Game of Friendship' had been printed in full in the Champions League Liverpool verses Juventus home tie programme. Six months later, after our trip to Italy, I thought of a final verse that summed up the feelings of many of us involved in this 'ministry of reconciliation'.

Let's make this game of friendship
A place for bitterness to cease
Where football takes the second place
To Christ the 'Prince of Peace'.

When I look to the future and sing 'With hope in your heart', it has particular poignancy for me now.

7. You don't know what you're doing

ROGER KNIGHT
Rushden & Diamonds

All followers of the beautiful game have experienced, and perhaps chanted, along with neighbouring fans, the words that
define this chapter. They are usually shouted out of frustration
that the referee is favouring the other team, that their players
are performing below the expected standard or because they feel
the officials' inexplicable decisions are spoiling the game. Similar words are at times directed at insulin-dependent diabetics
whose blood sugar has fallen to a low level making them appear
confused or even drunk. From time to time reports appear of
inexperienced police officers putting a diabetic who is suffering
from hypoglycaemia in a cell because that person is inebriated.
Without glucose the patient-cum-prisoner's condition will only
worsen. As someone who qualified as a referee 49 years ago and
has been a diabetic for 45 years, I qualify as a recipient of both
charges.

Top referees in professional football matches, and especially
in the Premiership or in international competitions such as the
World Cup, will often be exposed to far greater publicity than
a priest who usually works away for his or her entire life without much more than a mention in the local press when he or
she refuses an inscription on a headstone or has a row with the
organist. However, as is appropriate for someone undertaking
a lifetime role representing God to people and vice versa, there
is usually a more sophisticated and careful process of selection
of a priest or minister before the job is embraced. Once chosen,
trained and ordained, priestly assessment is a fairly recent
(though growing) priority in the Church, but falling far short of

the standards set by assessors and club secretaries who award marks for refereeing skills as they perform before cynical or even hostile crowds.

In 1957, Portchester Secondary Modern School for Boys in Bournemouth was a school keen to encourage those who had failed the eleven plus to take O levels and receive a good all-round education. In a town with a smaller-than-average number of grammar school places there was an incentive to stimulate late developers and those who may have had a grammar school place elsewhere. There was also a need to encourage boys to take up hobbies that they could develop in later life in the expectation that they would become fulfilled and useful members of society.

One such course offered once a fortnight on Friday afternoons, last two periods, was one on football refereeing. Although a rather shy and cosseted 16-year-old, I signed up in the hope that it might lead to a more consistent involvement in the game I loved. Until then my experience was that of 'on the bench' in games against other school sides. At the time I had no concept about what I was taking on and certainly no idea that nine years later I would be appearing in public in two different but unexpectedly related black uniforms.

Referees are necessary in football, as well as in many other sports, to enable the game to be played in the best possible way. Skills should be enjoyed by spectators as well as by players. The laws of the game are to be enforced. The guilty are to be punished and the innocent protected. If that sounds a bit like the way some people describe God, then perhaps we immediately find a link between chaplaincy and refereeing. In reality, of course, both roles, when they are carried out, are best done so in a less stark manner. 'Good refereeing encourages good football', claims the FA in its published *Laws of the Game*, and few will dispute that priests and ministers who function well are more likely to benefit the Church and those it serves than those who do not. Just as a leader of worship aims to help people contact God rather than the leader's own personality, so also a referee who is not noticed during the course of a football match is most likely to receive praise rather than criticism. The attributes (some, but not all, of which can be learned) of being a good listener with an ability to discuss what is happening, being decisive in clear decision-making, having empathy with those whom you may not know or have much in common with, and doing it all with a sense of humour, are those welcomed by both these professions who 'wear the black'. Having said that, even the shirt colours have changed since I started both jobs. In the Church nowadays it is not unusual to find a range of different coloured clerical shirts. In earlier days it was, after the manner of Henry Ford, black with just occasional grey, or purple for bishops – the colour never worn by a non-bishop if you wanted to avoid jokes about ambition. Now any colour is worn by the clergy to suit fashion or other accompanying garments. Referees, who in former times only seemed to change when refereeing in matches involving Scotland with their dark blue soccer shirts, now appear frequently in green or yellow because many teams wear black. Interestingly, I have not yet experienced a purple referee, but that may be because of the need to avoid foul language!

When an Anglican (Church of England) priest is ordained, a form of service is used in a cathedral or parish church where he or she is to serve, which sets out four key functions that the priest is to follow in the work that is to be undertaken. Be it in a traditional parochial situation as a curate and later as a vicar or rector who takes charge of a parish, or in a ministry in hospital, school, armed forces, prison service, or sports chaplain, the roles of *messenger*, *watchman*, *steward* and *searcher* are to be explored and maintained as essential guidelines by which to work. These key words are not to limit priestly functions, which often overlap or even conflict, but they form a useful template to measure activity and give the opportunity to explore the similarities between refereeing and priestly activities that I have been privileged to experience.

As Vicar of Naseby in the 1970s I found myself not only as the referee and team manager of the village school football team, whose six-a-side team in those pre-child-safety-in-cars days could be transported around the Northamptonshire villages in an ancient mini-traveller, but also as the locally elected district councillor. In a neighbouring ward to mine there was a small hospital scheduled for closure in the centralizing tendencies of the National Health Service to change structures in the hope that patient care may be improved. The councillor of that ward, being the owner of a small transport business given more to driving lorries and balancing books than presiding at public meetings, persuaded me to chair a packed public meeting in his village hall in front of the local press and TV cameras. We were in '*messenger* mode', setting forth a view that 'bigger does not necessarily mean better' and that people for whom services are provided have a right to be consulted. I found that the refereeing skills of authority, decisiveness and fairness were called upon that night. The messages were not heard, and the hospital closed completely two years later. For me it was a battle fought but lost. Interestingly, NHS Trusts are exploring the provision of enhanced health centres nearer to the patient with the help of PFI (private finance initiatives). Is the message being heard after thirty years or is it simply a matter of 'what goes around comes around'?

During this time, working in four parishes in west Northamptonshire, I was closely involved in public life connected with the proposal to build the M1–A1 link road (A14) across the site of the historic Civil War battlefield of Naseby. As the local councillor who lived in the centre of the village, I experienced the referee's feeling of being the only neutral person in the match when those who lived on the north side of the village wanted the road to go to the south and vice versa. I was also in a minority of local people who desired the enhancement of facilities to promote interest in such a significant battle in the life of the nation. The message has perhaps just been heard thirty years on as the County Council has at last taken an interest in that original proposal.

One of the most challenging refereeing experiences I had in the Church was also at Naseby, when my church divided over a far from uncommon vicar–organist dispute. Relationships can become strained between the parish priest who has ultimate control of music in the church and organists who are usually in great demand for their services and whose power base can easily become established on their supposed indispensability. When the priest is not musical and the organist's relative is feeling aggrieved with the priest's spouse, then yellow – or, in this case, red – 'cards' can be evident!

The situation arose when my wife asked a question of the church treasurer at the annual church meeting. The church treasurer was also the wife of the organist. At the next PCC (Parochial Church Council) meeting both the organist and his treasurer wife arrived at the meeting in a private house as proceedings were about to begin and placed an envelope on the coffee table in a 'we are indispensable' manner with the statement that it contained the resignations of both of them. Without further ado, and as is my usual practice, I thanked them for what they had done for the church since we had welcomed them and their family, and accepted both resignations. The Church Council was shocked. I was left to find another organist, and the church choir also resigned in sympathy and proceeded to sit in the congregation on Sundays. It took much time and a tense meeting of the entire congregation in the church before order was restored and the Vicar's decision accepted as correct. Had I been over-decisive in accordance with my refereeing tendencies? The 'red cards' which are sometimes 'asked for' by rule-breaking footballers had at least been confirmed, not shown, by me! I have valued the important refereeing insight that 'the *way* you give your decision is more important than *what* you give'. In the Church, what you do nearly always, and quite correctly, has priority. The priestly role of *watchman*, to ensure that individuals are not allowed to make themselves over-powerful and indispensable, is never easy.

In the words spoken by the bishop at an Ordination Service, priests are reminded that their calling includes being *stewards* who care for all people and events in the Church and society. In Corby, in the campaign before the 1984 General Election, I found myself chairing a public meeting on behalf of the Council of Churches in my large church hall, which was attended by all four candidates plus the local media. Corby was, and is, very much a Labour town, which, with its rural hinterland, had just become a new constituency. The Labour candidate was the current MP for Kettering, which had included Corby, and the Conservative was a bright young barrister fighting his first election and determined to win. Labour had switched their existing MP to what they supposed was a safer seat that they were confident to hold after the first five years of Thatcherism, but their candidate was 'old' Labour in more ways than one, with the complacent certainties of being a former shop steward in the then recently severely reduced steel industry for which Corby had been famous. With no sound system and only a gavel to keep control (I should have taken my whistle) I had to keep order, to allow a variety of questions to be asked and answered and to discourage a number of broad Scottish accents that really only wanted to shout down the Conservative. A riot was avoided at that nowadays unheard of event: the large, public, political meeting. I suppose I must accept the unintentional compliment heard by my wife which was shouted at me by a voluble Scottish woman, '[Chairman] Ye're wurse than Robin Day'! When the votes were counted on election day, the Conservative candidate won and held the seat until the arrival of Tony Blair and the demise of the Conservatives in 1997.

Little did I realize when asked, as the local rector, to be chaplain (Chaplin, as it was originally spelt in the match day programme) at Rushden & Diamonds FC *and* made an honorary vice-president, that I would become so closely involved in the running of a professional football club when the first generous owners gave everything to the fans in 2005. I had been invited to be an honorary vice-president when the new club was formed in 1992, becoming chaplain two years later when club officials admitted difficulty in coping with the widow of a fan sitting next to her husband who died after a heart attack during the match. Max Griggs, manufacturer of Doc Martens shoes, had spent £30 million building a state-of-the-art stadium and equipping a team that rose from non-League obscurity to the old Division Two of the Football League in eleven seasons, but they were unable to find a buyer who would ensure the continuance of football at the ground, Nene Park. So he and his son, Stephen, the then chairman, decided to hand over the team, stadium and 26 acres of land, together with £750,000 over two seasons, to the fans if a supporters' trust could be formed. It was an awesome idea, which had the support of a number of fans. We would be using the expertise of the Supporters' Direct movement, which had been set up by the Government to provide fresh and sustainable ways to run football in Britain and as an alternative to the 'carpet-bagging' failures that had often been evidenced.

The call to me came from the husband of one of the members of my congregation when I was Rector of Irthlingborough. Would I phone him? Would I do him a favour as the vice-chairman of Rushden & Diamonds Supporters' Clubs? The favour I was being asked was not, as I had expected, to take a wedding or bury some ashes at the ground but to chair the initial public meeting to set up the Trust. The Supporters' Direct handbook advises getting somebody well known for this job such as an MP or disc jockey. Rushden & Diamonds FC had to make do with their chaplain.

Three hundred fans packed into the plush Kimberley Suite at our football ground on 10 February 2005 to listen to presentations by the treasurer of one of the Supporters' Clubs. He had researched the trust idea, by the deputy director of Supporters' Direct and by the secretary of neighbouring Northampton Town Trust. They had been the first to pioneer a way of changing for the better the culture of football finances, which, over the years, has led to much heartache for directors and supporters alike. Questions from the floor included some from a person with a past dispute about the amalgamation of the original two clubs, but the meeting unanimously supported the concept of forming a supporters' trust. After this meeting the names of volunteers were collected with a view to establishing a steering committee to work alongside the existing board until a satisfactory take-over could be achieved. My own continuing involvement was proposed by a well-known fan, a Methodist minister, who had recently been transferred from Rushden to West Bromwich but who had accepted his new appointment on condition that he was within an hour's drive of our ground!

A steering group of 12 was formed, made up of people with a variety of skills but who in some cases had never met before. I found myself thrust into a role as chairman of those who were about to explore, to *search* for, ways to continue football and all its associated activities at Nene Park. There was even a resonance with the searching for the lapsed and lost that a priest undertakes. As with the Church, so with football supporters, attendance patterns are variable, but with one possible contrast – suffering leads to smaller crowds in football whereas in church hard times often increase attendance.

The football boardroom was new to most of us and I was impressed to find on the committee high-salary earners who worked in London and across the world but who on match days proudly wore their Rushden & Diamonds football shirts as they stood, often with their families, on the home terraces. The steering group also included IT experts, a retired human resources expert, a site foreman, the proprietor of a garden centre, a school cook, a legal expert, several accountants and, of course, a 'vicar'! We all gelled together quickly in the common cause of saving our beloved team and prepared our spouses and partners (not to mention our employers) for meetings on most evenings and for the proliferation of emails and telephone calls. Sub-groups were formed to engage in a range of issues from business practice to fundraising.

Just over two months after the Trust (Rushden & Diamonds Society Ltd) had been formed came the official launch attended by local dignitaries, including HM Chief Inspector of Schools who is one of our fans and who has the same name as one of our young stars on the pitch. More speeches were made and the Trust was launched by our manager, Barry Hunter, and children who are the youngest Trust members in a total membership of over a thousand.

On 3 June 2005, less than four months after the first public meeting, the Supporters' Trust took over the club stadium, the Sports and Exhibition Centre (on a lease), a number of teams and 26 acres of land in the Nene Valley beside the London–Glasgow A6 road. We could hardly believe what we had been given. We were excited, if a little daunted, by the challenges we had yet to face, but so far so good, and while all that had been going on we had (just) retained our place in the Football League as well.

I suppose I had been asked to be the first chairman of the Trust because I was quite well known to fans and the wider community. I imagine I was considered a safe pair of hands and I was a referee, too! I had begun the first public meeting with a sharp blast on my whistle. While remaining on the Trust board as the member responsible for links with the wider community, I stood down as chairman on realizing that others had far more business knowledge and experience, but mainly because of a likely conflict of interest between probably having to preside over inevitable redundancies and the need for the chaplain to stand alongside those so affected if they requested it. A large number of staff, not least a highly paid manager and some players, had already left, but the days of Max Griggs funding the shortfalls were well and truly over. Now the Trust inhabited a new world, which was one of responsibility and care for staff and the local community but, in particular, a world where every possible saving had to be made and income stream maximized so that football, and much else, could survive at Nene Park.

Everything was to be examined, including, somewhat bizarrely (as I thought then), the role of the club chaplain. For ten years my attempts to engage the club in discussions about the role of the chaplain had been met with a 'you just carry on, we're happy with what you do', and 'we have more important matters to deal with' attitude. Even my 'perk' as an honorary vice-president had never been questioned. But now I found my colleagues on the Trust board, with whom I had (as far as I knew) excellent relationships, were questioning not only my 'freebie', which I had already relinquished, but also, in the manner of the current culture of our time, whether Rushden & Diamonds FC should have a chaplain at all. It was suggested that I become a kind of social worker for the club. To be fair, many on the Trust board were unaware of the role of chaplain that I had been trying to develop over the past ten years, learning as I went along. So, supported by John Boyers, National Director of SCORE and chaplain of Manchester United, who gave me good advice and offered to meet the Trust board to support me, I presented my case for chaplaincy at the club. The outcome of this was summed up in the statement that 'while a chaplain can be a social worker, a social worker cannot and does not want to be a chaplain'. 'Who will bury the ashes then?' as I rather cryptically put it.

The result was positive in that I produced a pack about my role as chaplain of Rushden & Diamonds, which I delivered personally to the home of each Trust board member and then addressed the Trust board assuring them that, even if they voted to do without a chaplain, I would still remain a Trust board member and would most likely seek re-election when the time came. It was a relief to be confirmed in my role, and the proposal for this came from a member of the Trust board who confesses to being an atheist!

Most football chaplains find that their role at the club is fluid depending on factors over which they have little influence. They are appointed, not by a bishop or other church leader (hence in my experience it is difficult to find official recognition by the Church), but by those in control of the football club. The decision can be made by the board of directors after discussion with SCORE; a chaplain can appear on the whim of an individual club chairman with an interest in religion; or as the result of an incident at a match, as in my case. A change of club ownership or club management can obviously affect the involvement of the chaplain in the club, and the expectations of the functions of the chaplain vary considerably from club to club. They are inevitably determined by the chaplain's accessibility and the amount of commitment that he or she is willing and able to make. The experience of most priests and ministers in their day-by-day work of feeling marginalized by all but the church members is a greater challenge in sports clubs where priorities are essentially focused on winning matches and avoiding administration.

Chaplains who work in the secular world have to weigh up potential divided loyalties between being a representative of religion and their responsibilities connected with a job for which they may also receive payment. Unlike in a church where the priest or minister is a decision-maker with a historically defined role, in a football club, where the chaplain's role may be somewhat tenuous, strongly expressed opinions and unpopular decisions can soon damage the chaplain's attempts, in the words of St Paul, 'to be all things to all people'. This, of course, is an incarnational insight of being alongside everyone rather than trying to agree with each person we meet. Either way, a chaplain will find it difficult to be neutral in the way that a referee must be. The truth is that it is as impossible for a sports club chaplain to be neutral as it is for military chaplains to be neutral on the battlefield.

The service rather than the authority role of ministerial priesthood has moved a long way from the days when Church of England clergy were landowners, magistrates, councillors and the natural leaders in local communities, although some still are. When communities were far smaller than now, clergy more numerous and events, including sporting events, had little national, let alone international significance (after all, the Football Association was not founded until 1863), care and paternalism were part of the Church's function. Now that job descriptions are in vogue, even in the Church, faith communities respond in the hope that they may be relevant. Chaplaincy, therefore, has to be involved but, contradictorily, non-aligned. As a priest with independent tendencies, opinions to express and a desire for involvement, I find myself often walking a tightrope in this frontier form of ministry.

As a Trust board member, elected to run a football complex, I have to choose between the referee's insight of neutrality and the priestly job of 'alongsidedness' in my wish to ensure the survival of Rushden & Diamonds Football Club. I am finding that as a part of the establishment, but not the leader, I can just about manage to combine that with my role as chaplain. In the longer term, and certainly if the insights I am privileged to contribute to the Trust board were to be provided by someone else, I would return to a sole chaplaincy function. In taking this stance I hope that I am not claiming any unique contribution to my club but rather emphasizing the need for chaplains in sport in order that the beautiful game, and all other games, may not only become more people-centred, but may also raise sportspeople's horizons beyond success on the field.

Not only in the four experiences I have described, but also in family relationships prior to my ordination, as a chairman of committees concerned with changing services, ordaining women and reconciling supporters, not to mention umpiring village competitions in that most contentious of all games, rounders, I have been given the opportunity to encourage people to face facts and somehow to co-operate together to further common causes. I have had the privilege of being able to experience in a secular world and in a 'frontier ministry' the priestly functions of trying to serve as a messenger, watchman, steward and searcher.

Laws of the Game says that a referee's decision is final, despite frequent challenges to that by players, managers and especially football fans. For a priest it is, of course, God who decides even for the most authoritarian of our kind. Would there be greater similarities with being a referee if I had been a Roman Catholic or a fundamentalist preacher? Possibly. But the days when believers do as they are told are past, even for those who regret their passing. One attribute that Christians might learn from football fans is that passionate belief is good so long as it is within the law and with the greater good of the game as our ultimate goal. Would it really do much harm if congregations got as worked up about their priest as crowds do about the referee? But, of course, a referee is meant to be neutral whereas it is to be hoped a priest is on the side of the faithful.

So the two roles are different but complementary. Both leaders in black serve the best interests of those with whom they are engaged. The referee has to make instant decisions which are sometimes controversial. The priest consults, and with more than the two assistants ('linesmen'), before coming to even more complicated and far-reaching judgements. Both acknowledge that the 'beautiful game' belongs to the wonderful Creator. They are thankful to be given such a key role in activities that mean so much to so many and which have the capacity to achieve human, and therefore ultimately divine, fulfilment.

Referees who are priests or ministers understand what Bill Shankly was saying in his famous remark, 'Some people believe football is a matter of life or death. I am very disappointed with that attitude. I can assure you it is much, much more important than that.' But they also know he was wrong.

8. Who ate all the pies?

PETER AMOS
Barnsley

I recently heard about a football club chaplain who told the story of how he had been asked to go on the long-running, light-hearted BBC Radio 4 programme *Loose Ends* presented by Ned Sherrin. The BBC were going to do a live broadcast on a Saturday morning and had turned out a panel of sporting celebrities and enthusiasts including him in his capacity as chaplain to his club. The various interviewers unusually included a bright, theologically trained, former member of a pop group who was to ask him some questions. His opening gambit went something like, 'I can get my head around the doctrine of the Trinity, I can just about manage to understand transubstantiation – but how does a footballer's groin injury fit into God's grand plan?' Far from being floored (the chaplain had managed to sneak a preview of the questions in a relaxed moment), he found himself saying that in the grand scheme of things in this world with all its complexity and problems, the injury of a footballer, in one sense, is not the most important thing, but he made it quite clear that God is concerned about the small details and needs of everyone – even a top-notch player in the treatment room!

Not a bad answer I thought to a question that it is not unusual for chaplains to face from media personnel. Of course, that does not only apply to media personnel. My first experience of the home changing room at Barnsley FC immediately after a training session caused some raucous laughter. Stumbling for something to say to break the ice, I approached the chiropodist who was attacking the feet of one of our star players. Trying to appear interested I simply asked, 'What are you doing?' To which he replied without a twitch of the scalpel, 'Brain surgery'.

The whole concept of chaplains in the sporting world is still something of a novelty for media presenters, as one of the chaplains of Charlton discovered when interviewed prior to a live match on Sky. The interviewer had alighted upon him because they were 'always on the look out for weird and wonderful personalities in the world of football'. That particular chaplain hadn't the nerve to ask the interviewer whether he fell into the 'weird' or the 'wonderful' category. But the relationship between the figure of faith and the health and well-being of those who play professional sports is an interesting question that takes us far beyond the light-heartedness of the question posed here. 'Does God care?' can easily be answered with a resounding yes, but how God cares and in what ways God shows care for those in this world are slightly trickier questions. Ever since the tabloids ran their campaign for the nation to pray for David Beckham's injured toe before the last World Cup finals, I have been intrigued by what seems on the one hand to be a tongue-in-cheek attitude to faith and on the other hand a treatment of it as something of a last-chance saloon when all else has been tried for the injury-ridden player. It seems to me that faith and the search for wholeness and fullness of health have always had some link. For Christians, from the earliest days of their history, there has always been an interest in and commitment to healing and health care. Is it any different today? The question I want to ask, which emerges from that question, is whether there is a place for the chaplain in the treatment room and whether he or she has any serious role in the work of recovery from injury.

Injuries are an important and highly significant feature of any football club. Club chaplains see helping injured players as a high priority in their work of pastoral care at the club. We describe what we offer to the world of football as primarily a pastoral safety net – and that is what we seek to put into action. The needs of players in the treatment room are the most obvious and regularly occurring football-related pastoral situation. Often the mental torment is worse than the physical pain of serious injury. Questions are flying around, though some of them are rarely articulated. How long will I be out? Will I make a full recovery? Will I earn a new contract if I am seen as injury prone? How will I cope if I can't continue my playing career? How will I manage without the buzz and the acclaim? Will my wife or partner stand by me? Who are my real friends, rather than just the glory-hunters? On a few occasions I have felt it appropriate to visit a player at home following an injury (when I have known a player well and was confident that they would appreciate my coming and talking with them) or to go to see them in hospital. I have visited hospital on many occasions when a player, or other member of staff, has been injured or has undergone surgery. Many of them, having no previous experience of this, carry an anxious look as I appear, worrying that I have come to give them the last rites. Most chaplains in such private situations offer to pray there and then for the player, and it is something that is generally very well received. There was one occasion recently when one of our longest-serving employees was diagnosed with cancer and had to undergo emergency surgery. Imagine her delight and mine when over twenty other members of staff turned up to a prayer meeting at the club held on her behalf.

Some chaplains spend a lot of time with players in the treatment room. My normal weekly visit to the ground over the years, both at academy and first-team level, would prioritize those recovering from injuries. On the treatment table receiving ultrasound or down in the dungeon (the underground gym) day after boring day they are often glad of a listening ear. One young player who had been on the brink of a breakthrough to the first team contracted a virus that attacked his joints. He was in the gym almost every day for two years. The late diagnosis that came towards the end of that period saved his career. He fought off a pay-off from the club and the temptation to take a big insurance pay-day, never losing faith that he would one day play again. I still stand in admiration at his utter dedication and belief. We chatted together, trained together and occasionally prayed together. As a result, we are still the best of friends. His faith continues to sustain him. I have always prided myself in keeping fit, so spending an hour in the gym or running round the lakes was something of a pleasure and it provided company for those who found it simply a bind.

The whole work of physiotherapy and medical care has grown enormously over the last ten years. It has become far more professional and scientific and it involves a much larger team of people. I can remember when I started as chaplain there was just a single physiotherapist and a club doctor to cover the whole playing staff of the club. Now there are two physiotherapists, a doctor and a fitness trainer. Fitness and recovering from injury are taken very seriously and the people involved are well qualified and dedicated in their work. The space reserved for treatment, the facilities and the equipment have improved enormously and are far more sophisticated than they were just ten years ago.

Jimmy Armfield (nowadays a football pundit on the radio) refers in his book to being injured in the years leading up to the World Cup in 1966, which England were to host and of course win for their one and only time (to date). Jimmy had been voted the best right-back in the world after the 1962 World Cup in Chile and then got a dreadful and painful groin injury in a league game for Blackpool: 'At first, there were serious doubts that I would play again . . . in 1964, the only cure was a few injections, lots of rest and plenty of hope.'[1] He did recover slowly – but other people became established as England defenders and were part of the World Cup winning team; Armfield became just a squad member.

> I wasn't the first international to suffer a big injury at a bad time and I wasn't going to be the last. I was disappointed – but I could handle that. The possibility of being finished at 29 was a far greater worry.[2]

Jimmy Armfield is well known for his Christian faith. He is a lay canon of Blackburn Cathedral and plays the organ at his local church. His faith gave him a sense of balance and proportion that is certainly not universal in footballers of his or the present generation. There has always been phenomenal pressure to present a fully fit squad. In the avalanche of footballing biographies that have appeared over the last twenty years or so some have represented a view that suggests that such was the pressure that they felt injury was sometimes ignored and instead they were encouraged to present themselves as fully fit before they really were. For example, Norman ('bites your legs') Hunter, the former Leeds United and England player, wrote in his autobiography:

> I only ever failed a fitness test once and that was when I had knee ligament damage. Even then the Gaffer persuaded me to try a tackle, but Les Cocker caught me on the foot, my leg twisted and I was in agony. I told the Gaffer that was it. I couldn't play. He muttered something, walked away and didn't speak to me for three days. He was unbelievable really. Billy Bremner once played when he had a hairline fracture in his leg and, on another occasion, he had to carry on in a match after damaging his knee ligaments. Jack Charlton was shouting to the bench 'Get him off, he's struggling', but the call fell on deaf ears, whether by design or not I don't know.[3]

A player from the same great Leeds United squad of the 1970s, goalkeeper David Harvey, spoke of how managers need to use different approaches for different players: 'As a manager, you can't treat everyone the same. Some players need a kick up the ****, some players need coaxing along.'[4] A more recent player, Niall Quinn, wrote of how two different managers reacted to his having a serious cruciate ligament injury to his knee. At one club he informs us that his manager did not get in touch for five months after his injury: 'For him I'm just a dead man walking, or hobbling.'[5] Quinn then contrasts that with the encouragement and sympathy of Barnsley lad Mick McCarthy, as manager of the Republic of Ireland, when he injured his other cruciate and how he stuck by Niall.

Fortunately, this latter attitude is the prevalent one at Barnsley, where the present coaching staff, at the time of writing, have a policy of protecting their players when injured. It is also very easy to criticize managers for their attitude to injured players, but there is enormous pressure on them to get results and performances from their playing resources. The pressure comes from all directions: the chairmen and Board, the fans and the media. It makes no difference where the club is in the league. The pressure can be to win the Premiership, get a place in Europe, win a 'derby match' or avoid relegation, all of which have a major effect on the whole business of the particular club.

This is not just true at first-team level, it can even affect the academy matches (under 18s) with their league system, play-offs and FA Youth Cup.

In the past, routine cortisone injections may have been administered to players, which allowed them to ignore pain. However, in the long term this has contributed to major damage to the physical health of footballers and others who operate outside the world of football. Andrew Flintoff, the international cricketer, has written of how he struggled to fulfil his potential by playing when he was not fully fit. He had groin and stomach injuries for which in 2002 he took a series of injections to play against India at Headingley:

> Looking back on it now it was a big mistake: . . . I wasn't fit, didn't take a wicket, failed to score a run and I was in agony. . . . As well as the massive anti-inflammatory jabs in my backside I was also taking painkillers orally and if this episode taught me anything it is that I will never, ever do that again. . . . I think there was unreasonable pressure put on me to play . . .[6]

It is a fundamental Christian doctrine (an agreed truth) that we are all made in the image and likeness of God.[7] So, people should be respected and valued not just on the basis of what they can contribute on the pitch on match day. In the sight of God an injured player is as 'valuable' as anyone else – a Christian chaplain therefore seeks to minister that challenging truth, at a football club, a context where performance and results can seem to be everything. Injured players, with one or two minor exceptions, tend to feel totally isolated when unfit to play. Steven Gerrard of Liverpool and England was interviewed about his attitude to being injured at the start of 2004.

> You just don't feel a part of things . . . That's what I suffer from most. I feel as if I belong to the physios, and the players and staff are in a different place. You feel so down and lonely. It is, without question, the downside of being a footballer.[8]

This is a lonely place to be in, one in which confidence can suffer and self-worth can be at its lowest ebb. It is here that a club chaplain with time to offer pastoral care by showing concern, interest, help and compassion, all of which is important, can make a significant difference in the treatment room. Part of what we are there for is to remember that we are dealing with a person and not just an injury.

In many ways the insecurities that exist in players in the turbulent world of football become real and personal when injuries hit, affecting both them and their families. Those insecurities inevitably come to the surface. Even if they are never injured, those questions and uncertainties will eventually emerge at the end of their playing career. It is a bit like the human avoidance of the fact of our mortality – people try to pretend that they are going to live for ever; footballers avoid the fact that football only offers players a fairly short playing career. Fairly recently at our club we distributed to every member of staff, with the encouragement of both chairman and manager, Gideon New Testaments. This has useful helps, which include Bible references suggested for when someone is: feeling inadequate, ill or in pain, intimidated, just retired, needing guidance. Many have informed me that they are reading these and finding immense help from them.

People are all unique in God's infinitely varied creation. Thus I think that David Harvey's comments about managers needing to treat different players in different ways have particular significance. The management of injured players is a delicate skill for coaching staff and managers. For Christians, this strategy has a real and important theological foundation and involves what the religious jargon calls 'discernment'. This is a combination of logic, common sense and intuition in working out what approach will suit one person over another, and because injured players are in a very vulnerable state the process of discernment is very important. Some need strong encouragement, others need to be held back; some need a comforting arm around them, others might need challenging words. Chaplains are not club employees and so do not occupy their place in the treatment room by right, and so listening and offering encouragement are the principle resources they can draw on. Long-term injuries are often the most challenging and I have actually seen some players mature and grow through this particular sobering experience, as most of us often do through the challenges and difficulties we face.

Being with someone in this place of isolation is something that others have already seen the value of. Jimmy Armfield wrote out of his experience as manager of Leeds United that a dressing room can be one of the loneliest places on earth if you have to leave the field of play for any reason, whether as a result of an injury or a sending off. As an example, Armfield referred to following Gordon McQueen who had been rather dubiously sent off in the European Cup semi-final at the Nou Camp. Even though he wanted to stay watching every detail of the vital match, he wrote that 'Despite the pressure, I still followed him into the dressing room.'[9] The match was not his primary concern at that point; what was important was the way in which he showed remarkable concern for the individual player, his situation and feelings.

Niall Quinn described how he got the news of his first cruciate injury from the Manchester City surgeon Tony Banks, and speaks graphically about his own devastated response:

Mr Banks comes out with a big brown envelope, X rays and charts. Usually he's a jovial guy but he's wearing his grave digger's face. One word swims before me – cruciate. I've done my cruciate. No, my cruciate's done me. It's busted – snapped, knackered, ruined, bollocked, wrecked. It's betrayed me. It's done the dirty. It's sold me down the river. It's screwed me over.

Mr Banks is telling me about my cruciate, what it's for – what it was for, don't you mean? – what can be done? – a simple, tasteful ceremony perhaps? – where to go – back to the real world? down to the job centre? – the new surgical techniques – so they don't just shoot you?[10]

And there are some who are suggesting that injuries in football are more prevalent in the current era than in any previous. Hunter Davies, in his book on how football has developed and changed, writes:

. . . perhaps because of the lightweight boots and the speed of the game. It's hard to assemble facts . . . but I reckon that ten per cent of any team at any time is injured . . . And yet, in these days of large squads, they should be rested more, protecting them from injuries.[11]

I have no idea as to whether there really are more injured players now than ever before but if it is so then it lends even more weight to the case for treating the whole person. From my own fairly limited experience I would suggest that the figure of 10 per cent might well be underestimated.

The link between faith and the ministry of pastoral care is clear to me. I think it is also clear to me where I think the link between the ministry of healing and pastoral care and the context of the treatment room lies. However, in this area there have been other much publicized sources of assistance to injured players that some have tried to link to the Christian faith. Glenn Hoddle as England manager encouraged players to get help from Eileen Drewery, a faith healer, whom he appointed to his backroom staff. National newspapers reported unease among some England players who did not share Hoddle's beliefs. Club chaplains around the country found themselves in an awkward situation when players and club physios asked us what we thought about the matter. Chaplaincy is not primarily about faith healing in that sense but none of us would deny that we all want to be part of God's healing work. In a front-page article in the *Church of England Newspaper* in 1998, the Bishop of Chelmsford, John Perry, stated it was highly questionable to commend a non-Christian faith healer to injured players, and Dr Andrew Ferguson, of the Christian Medical Fellowship, warned that not all that passes for spiritual healing is necessarily Christian.

However, the place of prayer and the spiritual nature of every human being are features that are important to us and many of us as chaplains have on occasions prayed with players who are struggling with injuries, by the laying-on of hands (except where a groin strain has been involved – some things are best left to prayer from a distance). I could give three examples of players who were informed medically that they would never play again but are still playing regularly at pro and semi-pro level. Many others have received immediate benefit from this ministry. This kind of ministry is, more often than not, performed in privacy and confidentiality, though I can remember two occasions when I have offered prayers in the treatment room with the blessing of the respective physios who were also believers. The dramatic healing of one player was extremely significant in the run-in at the end of the season of Barnsley's promotion to the Premier League. I think, however, that in the use of prayer it is very important not to lend the appearance of being anything other than the chaplain who works with the other healing disciplines at the club and I would certainly not want to present myself as a healer. However, I do believe in a God who delights to make people well whoever they are, using every resource available. I have always had and indeed have encouraged utmost respect for the professionalism, skill and dedication of the medical staff. We work together and, hopefully, value each other's contribution.

Some players show a remarkable resilience and determination that is an inspiration to those around them. There is the well-known story of Bert Trautman (the German ex-prisoner of war) who played as goalkeeper for Manchester City from 1949 to 1956. He helped them win the FA Cup in 1956, despite breaking his neck in the final at Wembley against Newcastle. He was voted Footballer of the Year, the first foreign player to have the honour.

The same sort of resilience and determination is undoubtedly required in recovering from serious injury to a cruciate. Niall Quinn wrote about his recovery in his book – his work in the gym and of how difficult he was to live with – and adds a tribute to his wife's patience with him and support through it all. A player needs to show the most remarkable and single-minded attitude to operations, the treatment he receives and training regimes, to rebuild mobility and strength.

Another of our young players who was also on the verge of breaking through into the first team was struck with post-viral fatigue. He had been one of the most dedicated athletes in the club. It seems this may have worked against him. He was so fatigued that he could not even consider training. Blood tests were taken and came back showing up nothing. Devastated and confused, he turned to God. Through prayer, the resources of the best medics in the country and the application of immense mental strength and perseverance he ground his way back.

It was a long walk with many twists and turns: days of great elation and days of intense anxiety. It was often painful to see him as we walked through it together. He is one of the few with this kind of disease who has made a full recovery. After two years he got back into semi-pro football and is at the time of writing back playing professionally.

Quite clearly not all injuries come from the football pitch. In 1958 the appalling Munich air crash, involving the Busby Babes of Manchester United, was the worst accident to happen to British footballers in the twentieth century. Seven players were among twenty-one dead after the air crash. The British European Airways plane caught fire shortly after take-off with thirty-eight passengers and six crew members on board. The footballing world was reeling from the loss of some of its most talented young players. Roger Byrne – the captain – Mark Jones, Eddie Colman, Tommy Taylor, Liam Whelan, David Pegg and Geoff Bent between them had an average age of 24. Eight British sports journalists and several club officials were also killed. Sir Bobby Charlton was one who was on the plane, and was injured. He has spoken about his recovery, even saying he did not want to play again because he felt so guilty at his survival. His mother's GP, Dr MacPherson, in Northumberland helped him as he recovered. It was, of course, only 13 years after the end of the Second World War. Bobby spoke about what the doctor said to him: 'He told me that he had been in the RAF during the war and had seen his friends shot down repeatedly and that I had to learn to carry on as he had done.'[12] Bobby returned to Old Trafford, recovered physically and emotionally, and his career continued and prospered as he became a World Cup and European Cup winner with England and Manchester United respectively.

Players have to cope with enormous personal problems. I have had players talk to me about bereavements, marriage problems, friends committing suicide, homesickness, gambling problems, drink problems, anger-management problems and any number of more minor issues that affect their lives and therefore their performances. One of our players had a child who for no apparent reason would stop breathing. He would be rushed into hospital and spend days or weeks in a critical condition. The player and his wife would anxiously keep vigil at the bedside having to observe similar attacks that created feelings of panic, helplessness and despair. This player was booed from the terraces for his seemingly lacklustre performances. Even when I have tried to intimate that there may be issues in the player's lives that affect their performance the response is always the same. 'They are supposed to be professionals.' Understanding and support at times like this is vital for the survival of the souls of those involved.

Such support does not just come from the chaplain. There is a heart at many football clubs and I have been privileged to have seen the very best side as well as the worst side of football in my time as a chaplain. The physios are often the first port of call for the distressed player and I have enormous respect and admiration for those I have worked alongside. Some players are determined, disciplined and co-operative when receiving treatment and rehab, others complain throughout and many are totally unrealistic about the speed of their recovery. Their frustration and sometimes anger at being injured at all is often (though quite unfairly) directed towards the physios who are expected to show endless patience and have unlimited time resources. In a funny kind of way, theirs is an intermediary role in which they find themselves in a position that is somewhere between the health of the player they are responsible for and the desire of everyone else (player included) to have players out on the pitch. This mediator role can be a lonely one and it is one for which I have considerable empathy for in some ways I see it as a theological role. Not only does Christ's mediating role on the cross lead to his cry of desolation in the final act of reconciling,[13] it is one that the Gospels tell us that he faces throughout his ministry. Here is a figure who heals the sick and does good to people, who everyone else has lost patience with and yet, as the one who heals, becomes the object of derision. It is a strange paradox. It is also a lonely place to be. As for the Christ figure, so too for those who similarly find themselves in a different lonely place. In spending a lot of time with individual players recovering from injury, and sometimes apparently not recovering from injury, the medical staff also need support, reassurance and encouragement.

Physiotherapists are unsung heroes in my experience. Chaplains can provide the physio with time and space to let off steam and so act as an escape valve. It is great when players coming back from injury go out of their way in the media to pay tribute to the assistance they have received from the club's medical team, especially the physios. In my experience the physio is often a key and sympathetic person for the chaplain to know because he picks up so many vibes about people who would benefit from a chat with 'the Rev'. They are often people who understand instinctively the assistance of a sensitive and confidential chaplain. Indeed, it has been said that in some clubs without chaplains it is the club physio who often acts a bit like a chaplain in providing pastoral care. They are normally people who are extremely aware that footballers are more than just highly skilled, athletic physical bodies. Players, like all people, are meant to be integrated, body-mind-spirit beings. Injuries addressed in the treatment room have physical, emotional and spiritual dimensions. Chaplains want to play their part in attending to those needs in the world of football, which we believe God cares about. 'At times of great physical and psychological difficulty it is often the spiritual that gives strength and drive.'[14]

Compassion, sensitivity, encouragement and a listening ear are all needed in the treatment room, and so is prayer. None of us claims to do it perfectly, but these are people in the treatment room, not just a bench-load of injuries, and so we need to bring these attributes to bear in the search for fitness and health.

9. You only sing when you're winning

MATT BAKER
Charlton Athletic

If you can dream – and not make dreams your master
If you can think – and not make thoughts your aim
If you can meet with Triumph and Disaster
And treat those two impostors just the same;
. . . Or watch the things you gave your life to broken,
And stoop and build 'em up with worn-out tools:

. . . Yours is the Earth and everything that's in it,
And – which is more – you'll be a Man, my son![1]

It is the late 1970s and I am sitting in the headmaster's study being interviewed for a place at secondary school. So far all he seems concerned with is why my maths paper in the entrance exam wasn't as good as my junior school had predicted. Suddenly, there is a change of tack as the headmaster asks his final question.

'What do you want to do when you leave school?'

Without hesitating for a second I give my heartfelt reply, 'I want to be a footballer.'

In those days I knew nothing about interview technique and had made no preparation for this question. Had I known about these things then my research would have quickly unearthed that this was a predominantly rugby-playing public school, that not only saw such a sport as second class but also named the beautiful game with a word I had never before encountered – soccer. Nevertheless, I was honest and I still got offered the place at the school. I didn't, however, get anywhere near making it as a professional footballer (although there is a Matt Baker who keeps goal for Milton Keynes Dons).

Since that conversation, millions of boys must have had similar aspirations, some no doubt better expressed and many with greater cause to express them. For many these dreams remain simply that, but for a tiny percentage they become reality. In between the dreams of a 10-year-old boy and plying a trade as a professional footballer lies a whole gamut of other realities. It is towards the further end of this scale that the chaplain finds himself involved with the dreamers and the dream-makers.

As chaplain at Charlton, each year, towards the start of the season, I have an introductory session with the new first-year scholars at the academy. Charlton is one of about forty football clubs that have an academy structure, developing footballers from the age of eight onwards. Within an academy system, at sixteen years old, boys can be taken on as scholars for up to three years, during which time they hope to impress enough to be signed on as professionals. If they don't make it at the club at which they are serving their apprenticeship they hope that on being released they will make it at another professional club.

As I look at their faces and start to explain my role at the club I sense, and hear them state, their desire to become top professional footballers. I wish them all the best, encourage them and truly hope that they will make it. Yet at the same time I know how tough the professional game is and I know the statistics: 75 per cent of boys who enter football clubs at 16 are out of professional football by the time they reach 21.[2] I have no reason to believe that academies are failing; it is just incredibly tough to make it to the top.

Therefore chaplaincy to the youth players, while having similarities to that with the professionals, must have a distinctiveness of its own. It was with this in mind that chaplains at football clubs began to get involved with the Adidas football scholarship scheme about seven years ago. This scheme includes modules of core skills designed to help players at academies and schools of excellence to develop into more rounded people, and has been embraced in varying degrees by different football clubs as part of the clubs' programme of education for scholars. This is an attempt to address the failings of the past where an apprentice who does not make it leaves a football club at eighteen or nineteen with nothing to fall back on. Instead he now has the opportunity to attend college and take A levels and other educational courses as well as developing his skills on the football pitch.

When the PFA (Professional Footballers' Association) became aware of chaplaincy they approached SCORE[3] to write modules on pastoral care and personal relationships. Thus chaplains have taken on a role of teaching and nurturing by discussing such issues as relationships, bullying, morality, dealing with success and failure and where to find pastoral care and support within the club. While the scheme itself is no longer formally adopted as part of the scholarship programme, several clubs have continued to use the teaching in a modified form, with the involvement of chaplains maintained.

It comes as a surprise to many outside football that ministers of religion should be involved at this level, yet a glance at the history of football shows how many football clubs have their origins in church teams. Indeed, the singing of 'Abide with Me' before the commencement of every FA Cup Final is perhaps a reminder of these roots. Such involvement must be considered both a tremendous privilege and a responsibility. It is encouraging that pastoral care is at least acknowledged and in some places actively promoted with young footballers. There must be many definitions of what amounts to pastoral care but the following will suffice: 'Pastoral care is the practical outworking of the church's concern for the everyday and ultimate needs of its members and the wider community.'[4] In my experience I have seen how this can function in a prophetic, shepherding and priestly fashion within a football club.

The prophetic must include both a declaration, a telling out of God's heart, and a challenge to the pervading culture. As a society we have developed an attitude where we build up our young megastars one minute only to tear them down the next for not being able to handle the pressures and temptation. I recently read the following, which I found both challenging and encouraging in my role as chaplain to the academy: 'It's our job to prepare the younger generation to step in and take over. If they fail, we may blame them; but it may be our fault because we didn't train them better.'[5]

Thus, for the chaplain involved with youth teams, he or she can address this not simply by teaching a module, but more importantly modelling an alternative. A chaplain should be there when the team wins and when it loses, not criticizing the falling under pressure but being one of those who helps a young player prepare in advance. As part of my introductory session with the first-year scholars I get them to discuss certain imaginary scenarios to help them consider both how they might react ahead of time and how it could holistically affect their lives. For example: 'A player is badly injured by a dangerous tackle, which he felt was deliberate. He feels great anger and vows revenge. "I'll not let him get away with that." ' The discussions we have had in the years I have been taking this session have ranged from the obvious physical pain to the effect on an individual's social life; from the initial loss to a team to factions and a breakdown in team morale. Of course one 45-minute session is not going to solve every issue and no chaplain kids him- or herself that this time is the most valued by a 17-year-old would-be professional footballer. Nevertheless, it does open the way for an ongoing dialogue which will hopefully develop and deepen in subsequent years.

Here the prophetic image of pastoral care meets the more popularly understood model of pastoral care, namely that of the shepherd: Jesus the Good Shepherd, characterized typically in the images of Psalm 23, walking with his sheep, having compassion for them, guiding and protecting as he journeys with them. As the opening chapter of this book is at pains to point out, 'chaplains are the guardians of something that they deem as valuable', something most keenly felt in the care expressed to the most vulnerable members of our community.

It is important to stress that pastoral care within a youth set-up is not simply the function of the chaplain but is a responsibility shared with the other members of staff at the club. Particularly, in an academy structure, the chaplain needs to have a good working relationship with the academy manager and the head of education and welfare (HEW). The HEW is responsible for the ongoing development of scholars, overseeing their general welfare and educational progression. The HEW at Charlton, Phil Gallagher, understands the significance of the role of a chaplain in this context: 'It is crucial that the boys have as many neutral ears as possible to talk to and therefore having a chaplain who they are familiar with is vital.' I know that he values my input to the boys and is glad to have someone to turn to with any concerns for individual players.

In August 2000 our football club faced one of the saddest and most challenging times in recent history. While on pre-season training at Aldershot Army Camp, Pierre Bolangi, only 17 years old and part of the academy at Charlton, died in tragic circumstances when he drowned in a lake while on a cross-country run. From the perspective of those involved within the football club, Pierre's death was most keenly felt by the community at the training ground: youth-team players, first-team players with whom Pierre had recently been on tour, and the many backroom staff who had got to know him and watched him grow up from his earliest association with the club as a young school-boy.

As far as I am aware the club had never had to deal with such an eventuality before, yet I observed how it was handled with great sensitivity and understanding, from the directors down. While personally I found it a challenge it was also a privilege to be able to offer a degree of care to the many that needed to talk and be comforted at this time. In the weeks that followed I had conversations with those who were traumatized and those who were now reflecting on the frailty of life. A first-team player needed to talk because it had affected his performance on the pitch. Administrative and secretarial staff who missed Pierre's smiling face wanted someone to whom they could express their own sense of loss and confusion.

With regard to the other boys and staff who were present when Pierre died, the club provided professional counselling as soon as was practicable, within days of the tragedy. I spoke to the boys at this time, making myself available to them if any wished to speak separately, aside from the counselling being provided, and a number took me up on this offer.

A year to the day from Pierre's death we held a short memorial service at the training ground for all staff. I took this service and included a few words of remembrance, some prayers and a time of reflection. It was important for our community that Pierre was appropriately remembered. I know for some the service played an important role in helping them to move forward. In things like this it is easier to see something of the priestly function of pastoral care emerging, helping people of faith and of no faith to bridge the gap between their acutely felt humanity and the love of God in the human form of Christ who, because he suffers for them, is able to empathize with them in their suffering.

Not surprisingly, even five years on there are still staff at Charlton who are affected by Pierre's death, and no doubt his peer group who have moved on now will carry with them the effects of those days. Chaplaincy should not be perceived as simply being there for when things go wrong, it should be embraced at times of celebration too. However, it *must* function when disaster strikes, and I believe it plays a unique role at such times.

Naturally this chapter has been written from my own perspective, but I know that other football clubs have experienced similar extremes of tragedy when the chaplain has operated in a way that no other could. External help is of value, but there is no substitute for the relational context in which a chaplain operates. This comes as no surprise when we reflect on the life of Christ as the foundation of chaplaincy: 'The Word became flesh and made his dwelling among us.'[6] What this points up for us is that Jesus interacts with creation by *being* in relationship, by living out grace and truth on the ground amid the confusion, pain and joys of life. When the disciples feared for their lives during the storm Jesus was already there for them in the boat.[7] Doing and being as themes in pastoral care have already been taken up in Chapters 1 and 4. 'Do be do be do' was there long before Sinatra sang the words,[8] and as we see Jesus holding the tension between doing and being so chaplains must live their ministry in the same way.

The disasters faced by young players are not normally as extreme or as tragic as those I have just described. The challenges of caring for injured players are dealt with in more detail elsewhere in this book, but in passing it is worth mentioning the specifics as they relate to youth-team players. In one sense it is easier for younger players to deal with injury; the body will heal much more quickly as a teenager and, providing it is not career-threatening, it can be an important part in training for what lies ahead. On the other hand it is a lot harder: unlike the professionals on three- or four-year contracts they do not have the stability and security of knowing that their immediate future is being catered for. Furthermore, their time to impress and be offered a professional contract is of limited duration and a year lost to injury, for example, can significantly narrow this window of opportunity, as well as stunt their physical development at a crucial time.

The frustration is sometimes felt more deeply by those yet to 'make it' and a chaplain can provide an outlet for fears and concerns which cannot be expressed to employees of the club. Additionally, injury does provoke reflection on matters of life beyond football. While a chaplain is not in post primarily to discuss matters of faith I have found that both youth and professional players often reflect on the meaning of their lives while injured. I recall one occasion when a player asked me if the reason for his injury was down to God's judgement on something he had done. Another player found himself struggling with his own understanding of God now that he had been injured.

Beyond matters of faith, as we might traditionally define it, matters of life do come to the fore during injury, particularly if the injury is long term. 'What happens if I don't make it as a footballer?' becomes a more pertinent consideration when potentiality veers towards actuality. A recent television programme, *Life After Football*,[9] highlighted the struggles that many footballers face when they finish playing. Football can be very fickle, feeding a desire all the time one is young enough to play but leaving a terrible void when the body can no longer perform at this level. It must be appreciated that this was a television programme; as such, for the sake of interest and perhaps sensationalism, it emphasized a negative point. There are of course a lot of ex-professionals who have gone on to live fulfilling lives both inside and outside the game. Nevertheless, a number of players were interviewed in the programme who now found an emptiness that was difficult to cope with; pertinently, they had made no preparation for life beyond their

playing days. Of those interviewed Gary Lineker stood out
as the exception to the rule; he had made plans, thanks to the
advice and guidance of his agent, several years in advance of his
retirement.

The varying opinions of players and non-players indicated
the complexity of trying to address issues when the players'
focus on immediate needs (winning on Saturday) was in conflict
with their long-term needs (life after 35). However, the comments of Peter Kay, chief executive of Sporting Chance,[10] were
particularly illuminating for those of us involved in chaplaincy
with youth teams. He drew attention to the familiar scenario of
a young boy with talent at 12, who is taken on by a club and
then develops into a first-team player, earning vast amounts of
money by the time he is 17 or 18. The concerns he had were
quite clear: 'Nowhere in between, there or later on, has he got
a chance to grow emotionally, and that personality and that
dedication that is needed to get there are very, very similar
personalities and traits that we deal with in addiction.'

I mentioned earlier the attempts to bring life skills and life
plans into the curriculum of academies. At this stage, seeds
need to be sown both for those who will be out of the game
in five years and those whose career will extend into their thirties. However, for those of us who can remember being 17,
the reality of preparing for something which appears to be a
lifetime away, in any career, is a forlorn hope. In an industry
where performance sooner rather than later is paramount the
issue is exacerbated. Which is where, perhaps, a chaplain can
play a unique role during the times of a young player's injury.
A chaplain, who has the best interests of the individual at heart,
rather than simply the team, has the opportunity to address and
indeed introduce the subject of the future which hitherto has
seemed irrelevant.

Once again we return to the prophetic nature of pastoral
care, challenging a culture that can ultimately destroy by its
own small-mindedness. Phil Gallagher agrees with me in this,
being concerned that players do not become 'damaged goods'
when they leave the game. From a psychological perspective,
allowing for thought beyond the immediate does not necessarily mean a loss of focus on the present. In fact, on the contrary,

a more holistic approach at this point could increase performance rather than detract from it. Richard Rufus, the subject of a later chapter, is one player whose performances seemed to improve on the pitch when he became comfortable with his life and future beyond football.

As the guardians of something valuable, during times of injury to young players chaplains can help them to mature emotionally. Hopefully, through this we can at least turn some away from the destructive route of addiction. As Gary Lineker pointed out in *Life After Football*, 'ultimately it's about the individual himself', but perhaps through a caring and understanding attitude at these early difficult 'disasters' chaplains can help to motivate something of life-changing value.

In the more short term, excluding a career ending through injury, it is the end of the scholarship programme that provides the greatest fear for youth players. A few will be offered professional contracts; the majority will be released for trial elsewhere. As the time for decisions to be made approaches, usually in early spring, I begin to pick up increased tension from the boys. Some volunteer the subject for discussion, others need to be prompted and still others seem to all intents and purposes to be in denial of its approach.

At Charlton any player who has not been signed attends the Premier League release trials, which include within them second-career options for those not making it as players. I also make myself available after they have been informed if any want to talk, normally broaching the subject on a one-to-one basis with those who have been released, as well as congratulating those who have been offered a contract. Phil Gallagher takes a long-term personal approach to the situation, addressing an individual's needs as they develop as a scholar so that they can be ready ahead of time should they be released.

At other clubs the chaplain's role at the time of release is more proactive. While chaplain at QPR, Dave Langdon was involved with his club's HEW in putting together a package for those boys who were not successful in securing a contract at 18. This ranged from the practicalities of how to write a CV, to meeting with an ex-youth player who left the game at 18 and had gone on to be successful away from football.

The emphasis so far in this chapter has been on the 75 per cent who won't make it rather than the 25 per cent who will. Yet, as I mentioned earlier, we must be able to celebrate the joys as well as commiserating in the sorrows. A reserve or first-team call up, the signing of a professional contract, even the passing of a driving test are all successes experienced by youth-team players and must be seen as such. Indeed, *success*, in its original meaning of an 'accomplishment of desired end', is something to be commended. Charlton is a successful club, admired and aspired to by many for the way it has developed in recent years from a time in the wilderness to being an established Premiership club, as detailed elsewhere in this book.[11] Nevertheless, a chaplain also has a part to play in preparing young players for the trappings of success.

At QPR Dave always tried to help the boys to appreciate that at whatever level they played they would always be someone's hero. Money and fame are not in themselves bad things but learning what to do with them is where the challenge lies. At Charlton, in recent years, Tony Adams the ex-Arsenal and England captain has spoken to Academy boys about his own success on the football field yet paralleled failure in terms of a descent into alcoholism. Tony is very open about this, commenting in his autobiography, 'I was a footballer, a winner. But I was the winner who had lost when it came to alcohol.'[12] Nobody really knows what success feels like until it actually arrives, yet some preparation like this is vital and particularly well received when it comes direct from someone who has been there. From the chaplain's perspective, it is important to alert young players to the support network available, both family and friends outside the football club, as well as those inside, including the chaplain.

This also raises for consideration what is meant by success in our culture today. While I have already said I would commend its pursuit in its original meaning, many would understand success as defined in more modern dictionaries as 'someone who attains fame, power, wealth, etc. or is judged favourably by others'.[13] If this is the accepted definition, even subconsciously, then the dangers are all too obvious. A well-known, influential role model with a lot of money is successful, while anyone who does not achieve in this sense must be a failure. Where self-worth and identity are then grounded on such an attainment of success the problems for society are manifold.

It is not suggested that football necessarily does this but it can easily contribute to the problem. Indeed, as the most followed and in some cases worshipped sport in the world, there must be a responsibility within the game at the least not to contribute to and at best challenge such an acceptance. Chaplains can be a part of this.

From a biblical theological perspective success and failure are defined rather differently. Here we find them not so much defined in words as in actions, specifically found in the life of Christ: he who left heaven for earth, living not just *with* but *in* humanity, experiencing both the joys and the pains and whose 'fame' took him to death on a cross. Paradoxically, we find success and failure defined simultaneously in that one moment which stands at the turning point of history. Reflecting on this the apostle Paul could write:

> we preach Christ crucified: a stumbling block to Jews and foolishness to Gentiles, but to those whom God has called, both Jews and Greeks, Christ the power of God and the wisdom of God. For the foolishness of God is wiser than man's wisdom, and the weakness of God is stronger than man's strength.[14]

Living and working in a secular context this will always be a challenge. As chaplains we are not involved in a football club to preach this message in the accepted sense of spouting words from a pulpit. However, if such an attitude is in our hearts and in our actions we can do this pastorally. We can encourage values that are not simply about winning and price tags on people's heads. We can value people simply for being part of that humanity; we can espouse relationships above results and help people to enjoy success in the living of life beyond the 90 minutes. The wisdom of God and the power of God lived out will always find its adherents as well as its detractors. Once more I am encouraged by Phil's attitude at Charlton where he sees as much success in the number of players who have left the club in recent years to go on to university, as he does in those who have made it as footballers.

The poem 'If' is one of the most famous in the English language. The irony of it is that the list of conditions to achieve the success of becoming a man is virtually impossible to fulfil. The standard is unattainable; the ethical assault course confronting young people provides a test that everyone will fail.[15] I am sure that Rudyard Kipling did not have professional football clubs in mind when he penned these words but they are nonetheless pertinent.

Preparing, helping and caring when those two impostors, Triumph and Disaster, show their faces is part of the role of a chaplain in a youth set-up. I remember watching Terry Venables being interviewed on television after Gareth Southgate had missed the penalty that saw England knocked out by Germany in Euro '96. Amid the disappointment in the aftermath of defeat his reflection on how Gareth should deal with it resonated with me: 'What doesn't completely destroy you makes you stronger.' This is something that has stuck with me and I see its enduring application in the lives of young footballers.

Realistically I understand that my role, and those of the many other chaplains involved within youth programmes up and down the country, is not the most significant in the eyes of football. Yet it is valued and necessary to maintain a balance. That metaphor of the clown is a good one: 'Clowns, like chaplains, are not contributors to the national output, but they are commentators on life.'[16] Even commentators are listened to sometimes!

I was recently encouraged when I bumped in to a young player who had just been released by the club. We had spoken in the past about some quite deep issues, though not for a while. He spotted me and his face lit up and I could see something had changed about him. No longer able to fulfil the dream of playing for Charlton, he still wanted to find me to tell of a new purpose and direction he had found in life. He wanted to share his success with me, his fulfilment, and his joy. In no way do I claim the major part in what he had found, but I had been part of the journey, a chaplain had been a part in his success.

10. Going down; going down; going down

CHRIS CULLWICK
York City

'So, are you here to give the last rites?' asked the Sky news reporter.

The small car park of Bootham Crescent, home of York City Football Club since 1932, was full of the broadcasting paraphernalia of the assembled local and national media. But this was not the excitement of a big Cup fixture or an important League game. This was a wake.

It was late March 2003 and the club had been in administration since before Christmas. The press conference was promised at noon and after all these weeks in administration the club's condition seemed terminal. Now everyone was expecting to witness its last dying breath. The announcement the media entourage was anticipating was that the club would be finally pronounced dead and given a decent burial.

But I was not there to give the last rites. There had been occasions when I had interred ashes at the club. It is one of the things club chaplains are asked to do from time to time. It happens more often at bigger clubs but with no less devotion in the lower leagues. Ashes of loyal fans had been buried here, unmarked, over many years around the edge of the playing area. What would happen to them now if the club disappeared and all this became a building site for new flats or houses? It was a concern to many families who had already written or spoken to me about this.

Twelve noon came and went but no sign of a statement.

Things were continuing to happen behind closed doors some-where nearby. In the absence of anything else to report the jour-nalists began to look for some sort of proxy. One reporter asked if I would be prepared to answer a few questions and within minutes several others latched on to the same idea.

As the club chaplain I was there to . . . well, just to be there. Whatever the outcome of the negotiations with the administ-rators and whatever decisions were being made at that very moment, I felt that this is where I should be. Just being there can often be an important part of chaplaincy. I had learnt that much over the previous months. I was simply waiting and silently praying for some sign of new life, some hope of resurrection. Surely the delay must be a good sign?

One after another the reporters thrust their microphones and cameras towards me. That's when the reporter from Sky hit me with the question, 'So, are you here to give the last rites?' What had brought the club to this sorry demise?

The story has been well documented by David Conn of the *Independent* in a chapter of his book *The Beautiful Game? Searching for the Soul of Football*.[1] It is a story that has been described as a 'Hollywood script'. It is a story of the best and the worst in the human condition: greed, betrayal, passion and sacrifice. It is also a story in which it would be easy to paint a picture of good guys versus bad guys, when in reality things are never altogether black and white.

But this is a story of a club whose chairman and directors seemed to have engineered its downfall for the sake of personal gain; realizing the value of the land for development and pocket-ing the proceeds. They have their own account of their reasons and motivations but it is not surprising that they became cast as the villains of a plot which had all the hallmarks of a David and Goliath encounter.

York City Football Club has a proud history of giant-killing triumphs. Over the years it has enjoyed a number of famous victories. In 1985 York defeated Arsenal in the FA Cup, then held Liverpool to a 1–1 draw at home before losing at Anfield. The following season they again took Liverpool to a replay in the fifth round of the FA Cup and in 1997 beat Everton 4–3 on aggregate in the Coca Cola Cup. But no moment in the recent history of the club is more glorious than the defeat of Manchester United over two legs in 1995. York succeeded in scoring three goals at Old Trafford and then retained the advantage on aggregate despite playing a Manchester United side that included the likes of Eric Cantona, David Beckham and Ryan Giggs. Those were heady days and such memories last long in the hearts and minds of the supporters. They are still preserved in press cuttings on the walls of the club shop and offices. These same press cuttings decorated the walls of my eldest son's bedroom for years.

For me part of the magic of the beautiful game is the possibility that anything can happen. Whatever the occasion it is still eleven players against eleven players (give or take a few substitutes) and one ball. My first football memories are of just such giant-killing magic. Growing up in Swindon I started supporting the local team. It was the 1968–69 season and Swindon were not only riding high in the third division, they had the cup run that comic-book heroes are made of and every fan dreams about. Swindon made it all the way to the League Cup Final and the glorious twin towers of Wembley. Their adversaries were the mighty Arsenal who were then at the top of the old first division.

When Nick Hornby wrote *Fever Pitch* he recalled the day when his father took him to Wembley to watch Arsenal play a Cup Final game. For the young Nick the day was an unmitigated disaster.[2] For me, 15 March 1969 was one of the best days of my life. Swindon won 3–1 after extra time. What joy! I was 16. Now, more than thirty years later, as chaplain to York City, I found myself witnessing another David and Goliath struggle. However, this time David was not a lowly club pitched against a Goliath from the higher divisions. David was now the supporters of the club, who were facing insuperable odds to keep the club alive.

I was invited to become chaplain to the club in 1996. At that time York had a reputation for good book-keeping and living within its means. It had a thriving youth policy and there were a number of players who had come through its ranks and found their way into top-flight clubs. For example, young striker Jonathan Greening and goalkeeper Nick Culkin went to

Manchester United where within a season Greening had won a European Champions Medal and produced a windfall for York with his transfer fee and appearances bonus. The value of the transfer of the young keeper Culkin had bought York a new training ground. The sale of Richard Creswell to Sheffield Wednesday brought another windfall.

In 1993, with my two young sons, I had watched York beat Crewe in the play-offs at Wembley (although only after a nail-biting penalty shoot-out) and since then they had been enjoying a spell back in the second division. The club that had sought re-election to the league no less than seven times in its history was, in the late 1990s, well run and even profitable. Finances had always been prudently managed to the extent that its chairman Douglas Craig was often subject to abuse from the terraces: 'tight Scottish b*****d, he's just a tight Scottish b*****d'. There was in fact an irony here. Craig was the only chairman in the country who refused to sign up to the 'kick racism out of football' campaign. Never a favourite of the City fans, Craig had nevertheless served the club faithfully for years. But perhaps he was not as insensitive as the image he portrayed and he may well have felt that his years of dedicated service to the club were not fully appreciated. Douglas Craig OBE, JP, BSc, FICE, FI, MUNE, FCI, ARB, M CONS E had served on the board of the club since 1978. He had also served as a Conservative member of the local council and as a magistrate. Moreover he was extremely well regarded within the Football League.

In 1990 the former chairman, Michael Sinclair, was involved in a serious road accident while in Italy for the World Cup. It was an experience that caused him to reassess his ambitions and he began to train as a priest in the Church of England. In 1992 Sinclair sold his 123,000 shares to Douglas Craig, reportedly at no more than their nominal £1 each. Sinclair stood in a long tradition of club chairmen who never sought to make money from the club but saw the role as one of stewardship and a form of public service.[3]

But at some point it seems that Craig hatched a plan to acquire the assets of the club. This began with the formation of a holding company. At the time, this was defended and explained by the board as a move to protect the assets of the club from an FA rule which could be to its detriment in the long term. In June 2000 ownership of Bootham Crescent was transferred to the holding company BCH for the sum of £165,890. From the time the holding company was formed the finances of the club seem to have changed markedly for the worse. For whatever reason, by 2001–02 the wage bill had rocketed to 151 per cent of the club's income. York's financial position during this period has been described as one of the worst in football history.

Then on 9 January 2002 Craig made the statement that he had given notice to resign York City from the Football League at the end of the season. He also announced that the club was up for sale but it would have to vacate the ground and premises at Bootham Crescent by 30 June 2002 and relocate. He and his fellow directors would assist this with a contribution of £1 million. If a buyer should want to buy the ground as well as the club then the asking price was £4.5 million. On the day of the announcement the local newspaper, the *York Evening Press* wrote in a leader:

> York City fans have been betrayed. Bootham Crescent is to be closed and demolished at the end of the season, barring a miracle. Those responsible for its destruction are not faceless outsiders but the very people entrusted with the moral guardianship of this historic club, its directors . . . What motivated this unseemly scramble to dump the club? The four major shareholders who between them paid under £200,000 for their 94% holding and who stand to share a £3.5 million pay out are not saying . . . The directors call themselves City fans. Today they sold the real fans down the river.[4]

The supporters of the club were determined to do all they could to resist this and began to organize themselves. They felt that the club belonged to them as they were the ones who had invested in it down the generations since the move from Fulfordgate in 1932. It was they, for example, who had raised the funds to construct the roof of the David Longhurst stand. This was named in honour of a York player who died during a home game against Lincoln in 1990; the same season in which Douglas Craig had taken over as chairman.

A first meeting of supporters held at the *Evening Press* offices was soon followed by a first public meeting at the Tempest Anderson Hall in the city centre. The venue was far too small. I was only just able to get in. Many did not. Some players and some members of staff were there, along with hundreds of supporters. I realized that night that my role as chaplain had to be to support all those who were affected by this unfolding story; being there to support, encourage, listen and to play whatever part I could.

With support from the local newspaper and the assistance of an organization called Supporters' Direct the campaign soon resulted in the formation of the York City Supporters' Trust. This was officially launched on 1 February 2002 with an exciting and emotional event at York's Barbican Centre hosted by John Champion the ITV sports commentator. The Trust had been formed in record time. At its helm were a number of dedicated, determined and tireless individuals working to raise funds, to negotiate and to find a way forward. I signed up that evening as one of the first members of the Supporters' Trust and assured Steve Beck (a founding member of the Trust who was subsequently elected as its first chairman) that I would always be available to help in any way I could.

At first there was great hope that the FA would step in to put things in order. After all it was their rule that had been evaded. But it quickly became apparent that the FA either had no power or no interest to do anything. One fan organized a petition of six thousand signatures signed by fans of more than two hundred clubs. It was presented to FA headquarters in Soho Square, but to no avail. I spoke to the local members of parliament about what was happening. Questions were asked in parliament by York MP Hugh Bayley and John Greenway, the Ryedale MP who was also the club's President. But there were no answers.

'Save City' marches from the steps of York Minster to the ground gave an opportunity for supporters to demonstrate. Hundreds marched before one home game against Lincoln, including many Lincoln supporters and their mascot. It seemed to me that this was also where the club chaplain belonged and I did my bit, proudly carrying the huge red banner that would be seen again and again over the next months bearing the words 'Save City'. I considered it especially appropriate that these marches should start on the steps of York's wonderful cathedral; a place of prayer and worship for centuries, which speaks of the sovereignty of a God with a passion for peace and justice. I wondered if I should have offered to lead a prayer there. I am sure that I was not the only one who prayed silently on those steps. It is unclear when the phrase 'keep the faith' first became a motto at York City, but it did.

The question now was who would buy a football club in such a predicament? In fact the club itself was bought by John Bachelor. His name was not exactly well known in football circles. Described by the *Independent* as 'a former toilet paper salesman turned motor sport impresario', Bachelor bought York City Football Club for an undisclosed figure. It was later reported that he had paid £1. When he took over in March 2002 he promised great things, including a new stadium and premiership football. He also promised to work with the Supporters' Trust, to whom he offered 25 per cent of the shares and two seats on the board. Neither the shares nor the seats materialized. I met Bachelor on a number of occasions. He welcomed having a chaplain around at the club. His first words as I recall were, 'I'm an atheist, but I respect what you guys do.' I think I said something about anyone who was into racing driving was living nearer to heaven than me.

At first he could have easily been mistaken for the knight in shining armour. Not only was he buying the club; he announced that he would be buying the ground too. The fans for the most part welcomed him as the only saviour on the horizon. He presented himself as one of them; often watching the game from the terraces rather than from the lofty heights of the directors' box (where Craig had always preserved a respectable distance between the board and the fans). He would talk to the supporters and they felt he listened. Clearly he relished his role, especially when, at his first game in charge, he was awarded the 'man of the match' award! I am not sure how often a man of the match award has been given to someone who did not actually feature in the game.

But many wondered if he really was the man to rescue York City Soccer Club (as he now renamed it in the hope of attracting sponsorship from the USA). They suspected Bachelor was more interested in promoting his racing interests. Their fears seemed to be realized when in August, with the start of the new season, black and white checks appeared everywhere; the club strip, the club bar and just about everything else. The appearance of scantily clad girls on the cover of the match day programme was also not generally well received.

In the same month, Persimmon, a local property developer, made an application for planning consent for 92 homes on the site. It later transpired that they had already bought a 10 per cent stake in BCH, and that very little of a £400,000 sponsorship deal between Persimmon and Bachelor had found its way to the football club. It has also been noted that, around this time, Bachelor bought a house in one of the better Manchester suburbs. Steve Beck is reported to have said, 'He presented himself as the saviour and we felt betrayed.'

The finances of the club went from bad to worse and by November the club was out of money. Players and staff were not being paid. I remember arriving at the training ground one morning to be greeted with 'Have you brought the wages, padre?' It was no joke. Often here at the training ground players would talk with me about their own situations and the dilemmas they faced. They shared the concern of the fans for the club, but they had their own concerns as fathers with young children, partners and mortgages. For the time being they were supported financially by the PFA, but the future looked very uncertain, and if an offer came in from elsewhere it was hard not to take it seriously. They realized that their leaving could even help the club by reducing its wage bill, although it was bound to weaken the squad and damage morale. This was their livelihood. There was great uncertainty about what was happening and no one was giving any answers or assurances. Chaplaincy is fundamentally a pastoral role and there was a good deal of pastoral work to be done. One or two did leave at this point. Peter Duffield went to Boston and the goalkeeper Alan Fettis, a favourite of the fans, moved to local rivals Hull. How hard it was for the York supporters (and players) when their next away trip was to the new, state of the art, Kingston Communications Stadium.

Bachelor became increasingly difficult to find. He was 'away on business', and the Trust eventually decided that his position was not tenable. It was left to Steve Beck to tell the players and staff what was happening. These were the darkest of days for everyone at the club; it was just before Christmas. In the past I had been asked to organize a club carol service, but this year no one was thinking about carol services. However, I was often invited to write a chaplain's column in the match day programme, especially at the major festivals. So I took the opportunity to say something about the real meaning of Christmas as the promise of light shining in the darkness – a darkness that can never extinguish it. This was based on the opening chapter of John's Gospel, a reading that is almost obligatory at any carol service.

On 17 December the club went into administration with debts totalling £1.8 million. Bachelor's era had ended, but it had bought time in which the supporters had mobilized themselves and gained confidence. They began to realize that there was no one but themselves to save the club, and they had galvanized themselves into an energetic and ambitious force. Angered by the injustice of what was happening, and inspired by what had been achieved by supporters' trusts elsewhere, they became even more determined to 'save city'. But could this little David actually save the day against the Goliaths that seemed to be ranged against it?

Over the Christmas and New Year period the administrators kept the club in business on a week-to-week basis only through a fortuitous series of local derby home games and finance provided by the York City Supporters' Trust. There had been some interest in the club from one or two consortia, including an attempt by the previous chairman Michael Sinclair to put something together, but by March time had run out and the only offer on the table for the administrators to consider was from the Supporters' Trust.

As the administrators and other parties remained locked behind closed doors that afternoon the gathered media continued to await the promised press conference. But there were few to witness the event. Apart from me, just one or two young but lifelong fans were there in the car park. One told me he did not normally pray, but today he was praying.

Was I there to give the last rites? I desperately hoped not. I had done what I could to support and encourage those who had been giving so much so sacrificially. These last months had been costly for them and for their families. It had cost them a good deal financially. It had also cost an enormous amount in time, in sleepless nights and, in many cases, in careers and businesses that had been put on hold. But there was also a sense in which the whole city had realized there was something important at stake here. Many who would not normally have much interest in football wanted to see the club survive. Apart from anything else, York City Football Club puts York on the map. How would it be, listening to the football results on a Saturday afternoon, when York did not even feature? I had encouraged my colleagues in parishes across the city to pray for what was happening at the club and I know that many churches had been doing so. The prophet Jeremiah encouraged the people of Israel, even in exile, to seek the welfare of the city in which they found themselves. I found that as club chaplain I had a role both in expressing and in encouraging the concern of the local churches for the club as an important part of the community.

With the threatened closure of the club something of the heart and soul of the community was about to be snuffed out. The football ground might be more profitable to property developers, but there was something more important here than just capitalizing on rising land values. There was something here to do with the quality of the city's life; something about its identity and its links with the past that was important. There was also something about the injustice of the whole scenario that motivated local support. York City Football Club might not be the largest or most exciting club in the country, but it was our club.

The local newspaper, which had carried the unfolding story night after night, had played a vital role. The local council also had an important part to play. The club's staff had done far more than could rightly have been expected of them, and the players had given all they could in difficult circumstances, often performing brilliantly on the field despite what was happening off it. They collectively felt that this was the best contribution they could make. But the real passion lay in the hearts of those who had supported the club down the years, through good times and bad.

For the club to close, for this to be the end, would throw into question the meaning of everything that had gone before. Even the great moments, like the victory over Manchester United and the record 101 points as fourth division champions in 1984, would somehow be diminished, even rendered meaningless, were there to be no club left to celebrate its own history.

But perhaps the question 'What is it all for?' is just too difficult and too painful to face anyway. The big questions in life often are. It is often said that football is the new religion. For some it is the one thing that gives meaning and purpose to their lives. Our football heroes have become objects of worship; our stadia have become our cathedrals. Even in a city like York, with a small club and a relatively small following, football is part of the meaning of life for many of its fans. As one supporter said to me, 'I do not know what I would do when Saturday afternoon comes round; there would be a big hole in my life.' Here at the football club is the largest regular gathering of the local community. It is a place of belonging. The vision of the Supporters' Trust was not just to create a club that is supported *by* the community, but a club that is genuinely supportive *of* the community. They summed this up in the phrase 'building trust between community and club'. There are big issues here, including some big spiritual issues. The club's nickname, 'Minstermen', does not refer to any particular link with the wonderful Minster at the heart of the city. In fact the history of the club does not include a link with any particular church. But a surprisingly large number of clubs do trace their origins to the Church, and such links are sometimes still celebrated in their titles or nicknames. It is often overlooked how strong the link is between the origin of professional football and the Church. Swindon Town, for example, had started in 1894 when the Revd Williams Pitt brought a team together as founder members of Southern League Division One.

Bill Shankly is often quoted as saying that football is more important than life and death. Sometimes the club chaplain is called on to point beyond the passion and agony of the game to those things that are genuinely more important than life and death. Certainly at times of real tragedy and loss clubs will look to the chaplain to articulate something of this perspective. It happens at funerals and memorial services. Perhaps I would be called on to do something of this now. Perhaps I would find myself giving the last rites to York City FC.

Finally, the long-awaited press conference was announced. A brief prepared statement was read. To everyone's amazement the club had survived. It was out of administration and it was now owned by its Supporters' Trust! The gathered media circus shouted a few questions but received few answers. Turning again to me for lack of anyone else the Sky reporter asked, 'Well, what do you think of this? Isn't it just a stay of execution delaying the inevitable?' 'Perhaps it is,' I replied, 'or perhaps this is the opportunity for a resurrection. Perhaps there is room for a future and a hope. This is not just about a football club. It is about the heart and soul of the community. The club is now in the hands of those who care for it most, and who knows what might happen.'

So it was that, having battled a myriad of issues, on 28 March 2003 the York City Supporters' Trust completed its rescue package, and the Trust's new company, York City Football Club Limited, acquired the football business. I decided to try to pen something for the programme for the next home game, but not before leaving a bottle of champagne for the new board and a note congratulating them on all they had achieved. I also offered to do anything more that might be helpful.

Returning to my office that afternoon I wrote a piece for Saturday's programme. In it I paid tribute to all those who had worked so hard and given so much to bring us to this historic point: the supporters, the staff, the players and the families of all those involved. I concluded with these words:

> If we can continue to harness the goodwill of these last months who knows what the future might hold. . . . Easter is only a few weeks away. It is all about a sacrifice – about a resurrection and a new start. We know something about that. Keep the faith![5]

The following Saturday, York City Football Club welcomed Southend United. There were great celebrations. Once more I joined the fans marching from the steps of York Minster to Bootham Crescent, but now the giant red banner we had carried so often declared not 'Save City' but 'Save*d* City!' As we walked through the entrance to the ground we saw the hoarding had already been replaced. The black and white checks had gone, and it was once again York City *Football* Club. But there were still many unanswered questions. What about the ground? Would there be anywhere to play next season? Was there really any future?

On the Friday evening I had received a phone call from Sophie McGill. Sophie and her brother Jason had both played vital roles on behalf of the Supporters' Trust throughout the campaign. 'Thanks for the champagne! Yes, there is one thing we would like you to do. Would you please lead a prayer for the club on Saturday afternoon, on the pitch at half-time?'

'There is nothing I would love to do more, it would be a privilege,' I replied.

So Saturday afternoon saw me nervously taking the microphone and walking onto the hallowed turf. I was introduced with the explanation that the new board had asked that the occasion be marked with a prayer of blessing. But I was still nervous of the response. I had led a minute's silence here on a number of occasions, such as when Princess Diana died. But that was different. Football terraces are not always the most respectful of places. To my surprise there was total silence for the prayer and a loud 'AMEN' echoed around the terraces at the end. It really felt that a new chapter had started. It had. Perhaps it is still possible that Davids, with the help of the Almighty, can beat the odd Goliath. I could not help but think of the *Evening Press* leader back in January 2002, which had described closure as inevitable *'barring a miracle'*.

As part of the Trust's rescue package, over £500,000 of new funding had been raised securing the survival of the club. However, the lease for the use of the club's home, Bootham Crescent, was now due to expire in May 2004. A new battle was to commence. After months of detailed negotiations, York City Football Club successfully obtained a £2 million loan from the Football Stadia Improvement Fund and completed a deal to acquire Bootham Crescent from the club's previous directors. This acquisition ensured the long-term survival of the club. John Quickfall, one of the former directors, gave money back to the club. At the time of writing, the club are still inviting his fellow directors Colin Webb and Barry Swallow to follow suit. Douglas Craig is reported to have received £1,084,000 under the deal.

Despite securing a future, the club was relegated to the Nation-wide Conference at the end of the 2003–04 season. Perhaps there had been a collective distraction of eyes from the ball. The disappointment for all involved in the club was enormous. But having survived so much and come so far they were determined to bounce back. At the end of the last home game of the season, with relegation certain, the tearful team and board were cheered as if they had won promotion.

In early 2005 the Football Club offered the naming rights to their ground to York's largest employer, Nestlé. York City's Bootham Crescent home has now been renamed 'Kit Kat Crescent'.

The club is progressing with plans to move to a new stadium by 2015.

11. You're supposed to be at home

JEFFREY HESKINS
Charlton Athletic

It would fail because Charlton Athletic and The Valley were one and the same thing. It was playing in Floyd Road SE7 that gave the club its identity . . . And the past did matter. For there had once been a time, a fleeting span of perhaps fifteen years, when Charlton Athletic were a fashionable, successful club. Few of the people who made their protest that afternoon ever knew those days, but the memory was part of their Charlton nonetheless. Passed on in so many cases by fathers and grandfathers, the club's history provided the context in which all the modern dramas took place. More than that, the past was why The Valley was what it was.[1]

One of the strangest things said to me on a somewhat regular basis is the phrase that goes along the lines of, 'Of course, Vicar, I'm not particularly religious myself. My wife goes to church. She finds it quite comforting.' It is often the fate of the chaplain to be relegated in the minds of the masses to a compartment that is marked simply as professing faith or being equated with an official religious institution. The natural extension of this logic is to suppose that if you don't attend such a place – even for comfort – the chaplain is not for you and is therefore to be avoided at all costs. There will, of course, be some inevitable occasions in life when you will chance across him or her, perhaps a moment of great joy such as the birth of a new child, or of great sadness such as in bereavement when many others will feel awkward in your company. Generally speaking, however, the chaplain is not someone most suppose they have much in common with.

I suppose one of the reasons for this state of affairs is the way in which religion and the language of faith has become locked up in religious faith buildings. In an increasingly secular context and a culture of individualism where you do your thing and I do mine, both faith groups and the prevailing culture have some responsibility for this situation. It is deemed all right to do the God stuff behind sacred walls, but when it emerges from there it is met with an awkwardness that is itself a challenge. This is where the whole notion of chaplaincy, which is visibly the growth area of ministry in the current age, has to reinvent itself. We are back to the concept of doing and being found in Chapter 1. What we are determines what we do, and what we do shapes the way in which we see ourselves.

Perhaps a second reason might be the way we make use of religious language. There is something rather elitist about some religious language, and elitism either alienates or invites ridicule. So the time-worn joke, 'Jesus saves, but Keegan knocks in the rebound', is one example of that, while the glazed looks of the crowds going to the game to be lambasted by the young man with his text-filled sandwich boards and his megaphone posing the question 'Why be sinners when you can be winners?' is another. What are we doing with our God-talk when we offer images like that?

The word 'religion' is often passed over now in favour of the word 'faith', or even 'spirituality', which I think is a bit of a shame. There are some academic scholars who have done research on this, and it is clear from their investigations that the word 'religion', for many people, is equated with either belonging to a religious institution or organization[2] or signing up to a set of regulations or beliefs.[3] The researchers also tell us that terms like 'faith' or 'spirituality' have, in the current era, adopted a more liberating feel. Faith can be personal and experiential, they say, whereas being religious suggests, for many, a sense of adherence or subjection to the authority of an ecclesial or other organization. It might be true that what people mean by not being religious means that they don't attend church, mosque or synagogue, but I think that the three terms are themselves interconnected while being quite different. For me it is the football fans that have pointed the way; even those who aspire to being 'not particularly religious myself' are often those who will also dare to say the unthinkable, 'Following this team isn't a hobby – it's a religion!' Now, in a culture where spirituality is in and religion is supposedly not, where did that come from?

The cynic might deem this at best a heresy, passing off religion as an obsessive kind of fundamentalism for the immature football fan, but I think that we might be rather more generous. The word 'religion' as we have it appears to find its source in the Latin word *religare*, meaning to tie something, as in making some kind of obligation. From it we get words like 'rely' and 'reliable'. In the course of time it came to describe the relationship between human beings and those things that they held as sacred – ultimately God. It does not describe any kind of personal relationship with God, in the sense of a personal conversion experience, but it does nonetheless tell us something important about human beings. Human beings are not innately creatures that live in isolation from one another. Relationships are important; some relationships are of particular significance, and some so particularly significant that they are described in terms of bonding. Early contact between a newborn child and its parents effects a bonding that hopefully grows into a relationship of trust and commitment – a kind of tie or fusion between people that grows with time.

Football fans don't need to be told this. They know it implicitly. Following a team or supporting a club can in that way be a kind of religion. There is a bond or fusion that grows without being seen until someone tries to remove it. Then it reveals an awesome power of resistance. If you can understand this, you will understand why football fans revere the home of their allegiance – the stadium.

> At the heart of each soccer tribe lies its street temple, the stadium. So strong is its magic that for a tribesman to approach it, even on a day when there is no match, creates a strange feeling of mounting excitement. Although it is deserted he can sense the buzz of the crowd and hear again the roar of the fans as the ball hits the back of the net. To a devoted tribesman it is a holy place, with a significance that is hard for an outsider to appreciate.[4]

Charlton Athletic Football Club is what we call a split-site club. The training ground and the stadium are a good five miles away from each other. So, we offer two chaplains. Matt Baker goes to the training ground and makes contact with players and staff alike, and I spend some of my time at The Valley stadium. I truly love the lot that I have drawn in our chaplaincy team, for it reminds me that football clubs are not all about the squad that gets picked to play. In addition, they have to embrace, not only the support staff and ancillary workers, but also the caterers, ground staff and security guards, receptionists, ticket sales staff, and a whole host of others. When you come into contact with any aspect of the supporters club, Junior Reds and community development, you immediately come into contact with the memory of the ancestors – the heroes and villains who made the story what it is thus far. The passion of true religion is revealed in the way that the faithful tell the story that is theirs and pass it on to others. Anyone who has been a part of a faith community knows that to be true.

In the London Borough of Greenwich, in the historic parish of Charlton, the ancient parish church where I am rector sits at the top of the hill overlooking the River Thames. It has been there in some shape or form for the best part of a thousand years, and when you wander inside a good deal of its history is reflected in the monuments and tributes that adorn its walls. There is a bust and memorial to the late Spencer Percival, Prime Minister in the early nineteenth century, who was assassinated by a man who had been ruined as a result of his economic policies. There is a memorial to the late Master Edward Wilkinson, chief cook to Her Majesty Queen Elizabeth I. He was known as the Yeoman of the Mouth! There are numerous tributes to the military men who emerged from the nearby Woolwich barracks. They all contribute to a story that belongs to the community that lives and worships there.

If you wander down the road towards the Thames, you will find, nestling in the valley, the football stadium that is its namesake. It has been there for the best part of a hundred years, and it too has a story that is punctuated by the monuments and memorials of its past. As you walk in through the main gates you are met by a towering figure with a shock of hair piled high on his head. This is Sam Bartram, legendary goalkeeper who (having made a club record of 623 appearances) has passed into local footballing folklore as gentle man and distinguished athlete. That memory is now preserved in a magnificent bronze casting, which stands at the main entrance greeting the faithful as they arrive. There are still people around here who remember him. Inside the main entrance is a bust of the most successful manager in the club's history. Jimmy Seed saw them promoted through successive divisions and took them to two Cup Finals after the war, winning the second in 1947. It was a remarkable period in the life of Charlton Athletic and one that Bartram himself recorded in anecdotes that became legend.

> The 1946 final was not one of the greatest on record . . . About ten minutes from time our right-half, Bert Turner, had one of the most agonising experiences it is possible for a player to undergo in a Cup Final – he put the ball through his own goal . . . Within minutes, however, he had made amends. Entrusted with a free kick, he shot hard and low. The ball came to rest snugly in the Derby net. Bert had scored two goals – one for each side!
>
> So we came to extra time, level at one goal each, but in this period County found their top form, overran us, and deservedly won 4–1 . . .
>
> Back in the dressing room we were naturally dejected. To be on the losing side in the Final is an unhappy climax to all those weeks of preparation and anticipation; and not a single smile relieved the gloom when someone said with forced cheerfulness: 'Never mind, lads; we'll be here next year – and we'll win.' I can't remember who the prophet was. But he proved to be absolutely right.[5]

These anecdotes become part of the wider story, and telling that story is important. The heroes that mould our communities are key figures and should not be forgotten, for they shape the lives of those who follow but who will never have a monument or a statue in their memory. All of this is deeply religious, for it ties us willingly to a past and in so doing challenges us to meet the future.

Yet all of this might have been lost had others (who have

not been cast in bronze and are unlikely to be) got their way. For there was a time of exile for this club when the movers and shakers deemed to take the masses from their homeland to a strange land, and in so doing revealed just how important a sense of home is for the football fan as for anyone else. In September 1985, the fans watching Charlton beat Crystal Palace 3–1 at The Valley were told by the then club chairman John Fryer that the club was moving to share the stadium and facilities at Selhurst Park. The final home game to be played would take place on 21 September. That turned out to be a game remembered more for the protests that took place than for any football. Fans invaded the pitch at half-time and laid wreaths in the centre circle. They occupied the centre of the pitch until the manager came out to ask them to allow the game to continue. Passionate about the very thing they were losing, but appearing confused and uncertain about what to do, they showed all the signs that we see in pastoral ministry when we come across loss and grief.

The effect of the time of exile at Selhurst Park was to do for the faithful what the owners can never have imagined. For those who made the trip it became a time of coming to terms with the reality of the loss and of dealing with their grief in the way that many do: organize; strategize and campaign. All death is tragic to those who share in the grieving, but there are those occasions when it can seem particularly so. The death of a child from a dreadful illness can see charitable campaigns established to purchase hospital equipment or fund research. Innocent victims of violence will often inspire peace movements, which catapult the grieving relatives into a very public and often political response to their loss. In this instance the loss and grief was of a different kind. It involved a huge community, which had been forced to experience displacement with no apparent consultation. The landlords had served an eviction order on the community and, as if to add insult to injury, had carried them away to another place, stripping them of the key characteristic of their identity, namely their home and the place to which they had a sense of belonging. The result was a rediscovery of the self and the ability to empower that self through protest.

For those years in exile, 'The Valley is our home' became

the mantra phrase of the faithful who went to Selhurst, and also of those who refused to go. What grew among them was a belief that they might change things. They came to do this in the local elections for Greenwich Borough Council on 3 May 1990. Having tried to negotiate a return to The Valley, and seeing their planning application for the stadium turned down by the Borough Council, 'homeless of Charlton' suspected a conspiracy at the Town Hall; in response, they formed a political party to fight them at the ballot box.

The Valley Party lived for this one election only and fought its campaign on the single issue of the right to return to The Valley. With few resources and little experience in such campaigns, these football fans turned political activists became, in my view, a remarkable icon in political history. The party won no seats, but took almost 11 per cent of the votes polled throughout the borough. In certain wards, they took sufficient bites out of the traditional Labour vote to cause serious anxiety to the sitting Labour councillors. In the Eynsham ward, Councillor Oelman, who had chaired the planning committee that had turned down Charlton's application, lost his seat, as did his running mate. It was a defining moment in the history of the club. From that moment the displaced community who had begun life as a group of protesters occupying the centre circle of their beloved home ground in 1985, grieving and uncertain as to what to do next, had become a formidable force for change. They were being taken seriously. In little more than a year Greenwich Council had given the green light for the fans to return home.

Wendy Perfect became a kind of convert to football and was someone who saw quite quickly the importance of the local place with the playing of the game. Now a club employee, she traces her fondness for the place to the time when she stood for the Valley Party at that election and remembers how it changed things for her. As a result of this experience she saw the importance of its existence as a place that was 'home' for the football-supporting community within a wider local community.

I like the way this club values being part of the community and I find that I appreciate the friendships that I have made through football. I like the banter and the togetherness that exists between the supporters. I have realized for a long time that football is a great leveller, no matter what your station in life.

The great levelling factor here was the way in which everyday people from all those different stations in life were galvanized into action because of their grief. It became an issue of political injustice.

> It was at this time that I got involved with the campaign to get them back to The Valley. It was a political issue that did what politics should do – bring people together. I didn't know many people at the football club at the beginning but our common defining factor was that we didn't want this important thing in our lives to die.

What happened seems to have been a moment of realization. Other people were on their side too. Silent voices began to offer their support. There was a groundswell of indignant resentment that perceived (rightly or wrongly) the political servants of the borough as the cause of their grief. The more oppressed they felt, the more they grew in stature and confidence.

> There was a public meeting at Woolwich Town Hall and the place was packed but everyone felt that the decision [to turn down the planning application] had been made before we ever got to the meeting. It was a charade, but it only strengthened our resolve at every level. During the campaign all the supporters got involved in the leafleting and because of that we discovered what local people thought. Nobody was anti-Charlton and all we got was loads of sympathy from people who followed Arsenal and others who said to us that Charlton belong at the Valley. It was a fantastic campaign.

Charlton returned to play football at The Valley on 5 December 1992, an important date for any who took part in that campaign. One complete side of the ground remained bare as fewer than ten thousand people packed into what was available for use to see the exiles return to beat Portsmouth by a solitary Colin Walsh goal to nil. It was a remarkable return and one that has distinct religious themes to it. Wendy recalls: 'We remembered the return to The Valley by having a dinner. It went on for the first ten years but it doesn't happen now.' I attended these dinners. I thought they were important events of social memorial. They were great events, often attracting a good speaker, but something was missing. On one occasion I stood at the bar next to two first-team players who were in conversation with each other. One asked the other what the dinner was in aid of, and the other said that he didn't know but clearly it was important to the fans. Here, I think was the clue. We had missed something of religious significance. This is what I mean.

I love this story of the return to The Valley and how it came about. I often tell it to people I meet, and find myself feeling a sense of pride in the telling. It resonates for me at a much deeper level as a human being, for it is a story that has some universal traits. It makes me remember things that are not my memories at all, but those of other communities, which have been retold time and again, but which have become important to me because of the connections that I find in them. So for example, whenever I think of this story or find myself telling it, I make connections with the biblical account of the exile, so important to Jews celebrating Passover, or Christians setting their Easter story in its context. Many of the themes I find in it are similar. A community is displaced and begins to feel oppressed. It gathers itself to lament its situation. A leadership emerges to challenge those in positions of perceived power. The community discovers its own voice and begins to protest. Those occupying positions of perceived power become threatened and defensive. The community protest gathers momentum and eventually wrestles back power of its own to change its future. The community journeys from the place of exile, through the nomadic period of uncertainty, to the place it calls 'home'. The community celebrates its arrival and vows never to forget the ordeal, knowing that it has discovered what it means to be free.

When Jews meet to celebrate Passover their reason for so doing is to remember the price of freedom. Their very act of remembrance is made through a ritual re-creation of the events that we call the Exodus. In it, each member of the family takes a part in the telling of the story and all present eat foods that remind them of the same. Christians understand this as the set-ting for their celebration of Easter. Jesus is the new Exodus whose death is transforming of the community that has come to surround him. Whatever else is understood by the events of Passover or the resurrection that is Easter, one thing is clear: the participation in retelling the story is critical, for if the story is not remembered, it is lost and is unlikely to be recovered by the community to which it belongs. I think it is for that reason that I am sad that the celebration of this particular event in the life of the football club has come to an end. All the ingredients were there. The dinner always took place in the stadium over-looking what has now become a transformed Valley; many of those who had participated in restoring the fortunes of the club and making the move home again were in attendance, so the context was set.

Remembering can sometimes be confused with sentimental-ity or nostalgia, but it is not the same. Remembering is a way of re-entering a story of the past in order to live differently in the present. Somehow, remembering is designed to move us on in human living. It is part of the fusion or tie that the word 'reli-gion' really has for us. Remembering the past is not the same as living in it, but it is a common human characteristic to equate the one with the other. To that extent, acts of true remembrance can often be painful ones, even when the outcome or the greater good was served by it. So, it is not unusual still to see veterans of the world wars weep at the recollection of the friends that they lost in human conflict, even though the friendships that were fostered have remained intact in their memories. They live the story by retelling it, and it is clear in the telling that some have moved on much further than others.

So, we have a plaque at The Valley stadium commemorating those who fought in the election, but how I wish we were still telling the story in some living way! Of course you will say that the story has been preserved because I have written about it here, and others have done so in far greater detail, but reading and telling are only cousins in the same family. They have simi-lar characteristics, but they do quite different things.

When I take a funeral service I am often asked to say some-thing about the person who has died even though I may be the only person present who never knew the deceased at all. I always ask the family if they would like one of their number to speak, but nine times out of ten they will decline on the grounds that it would be too emotional for them. It is really quite understandable and I am touched by the faith that they have in me to do this for them. What we then have to do is to piece together the story of the person that they loved, so that I can tell it for them while they are unable to. There are times in life when as ministers of religion we are asked to stand in the cavern of someone else's grief and hold the story for them. There are times when we are asked to do that for entire communities too.

Chaplains need to see themselves as the guardians of the community story. They should not be guardians in a miserly and possessive way, keeping the story to themselves and bringing it out to entertain and impress when it suits them. A true guardian cares for the story but also has a responsibility to enable the real inheritors of that story to grow up wanting to discover it and tell it for themselves. Unless there is someone to hold that story, the past and those who lived its events become forgotten. To be forgotten must be one of the greatest human tragedies.

For that reason the choice of a last resting place for those who have died is deeply significant to the act of remembering. Football stadiums have become a part of that remembering culture for many of its followers. It is the place of homecoming for many of them and underlines the value of what it means, not only to play at home, but also be at home for the modern football fan.

One of the first official duties I ever performed as a football club chaplain was to scatter the cremated remains of a long-serving loyal fan. He had been a turnstile operator and raffle ticket seller. He and his wife hardly missed a game, home or away, and it was on one of these travels as he followed the fortunes of his team at an away game in the north east that he suffered a heart attack and died. The Valley was his home, his widow told me when I met her, and it was his request that it be his final resting place. The club had agreed and the affection with which the ground staff held him was apparent in their behaviour on the day we came to scatter his ashes. It was a quite remarkable experience and one that I often recollect when I find the sincerity of football fans brought into question. Without any prompting from me, we left our meeting point at the main reception desk in silence and spontaneously got into a kind of liturgical formation. The head groundsman led the procession like an undertaker, while I led the chief mourners bearing the box with his ashes in. The cleaning staff were on duty that day sweeping up the debris left after Saturday's game. As we entered the stadium they all stopped and stood to attention, brooms to one side, as if offering a guard of honour, and they remained like that until his memory had been marked with a customary silence. It was an event that was to challenge our thinking when similar requests began to come in. This stadium was a place of such significance; the man's family had described it as home and now they had brought him home to the place where he had shared his best memories. We would have been fools if we had not taken note of that and acted upon it. Fortunately, thanks to a conversation between the club secretary, the club grounds-man and the club chaplain, we were able to anticipate what was to follow.

Nowadays, in one corner of The Valley stadium, between the east and the south stand, there is a small memorial gar-den. Its size and simplicity belies its significance, as has become apparent over the years. Moving the idea of such a place was in anticipation of what soon became a growing number of requests for the cremated remains of loyal and devoted fans to be scat-tered on the football pitch. The sheer volume of requests could not be met practically while still looking to maintain a decent playing surface! All welcomed my suggestion for a memorial garden, and the plan was implemented within weeks of suggest-ing the idea. What I found particularly touching was the com-mitment to openness. This would be a special place that people could openly see and not something tucked away in a corner. The garden would be set within the stadium itself. To this day, that has been something that has been most appreciated and admired by those coming to use it. Since its inception, nearly a hundred families have made use of it as a practical place to leave the mortal remains of their deceased loved ones, and, perhaps more importantly, as a place to lodge their memories. At the moment, the site overlooks the south goal, inspiring comments like, 'Well, he will never have to buy another season ticket again', or, 'Rest in peace and may you see more home goals this season than last!' Then there are the suggestions that the deceased will be more influential upon the outcome of future games from beyond the grave than ever they were from their seat in the stands in life! The comments always make me smile, as people often do when they wrestle for a language that speaks to them through the mystery of death about life itself. In a way I think that making space for people to talk about these important things is what chaplaincy is all about and is the very thing that most people in the busy and fast moving world of football find too little time for.

Colin Powell, signed from non-league Barnet for Charlton in 1973 (a bargain at £7,000), remembers his first goal against Blackburn at home (left-footed – quite unusual) and is now the head groundsman. He has seen the fortunes of the club fall and rise, the stadium change beyond recognition, and the advent of the modern game with a professionalism that exists at every level of club life. He is also a man who knows that the world of professional football always risks becoming impersonal. For him the personal touch is the human face of a football club. There was no chaplain at the club when he first joined, and sometimes he wishes that there had been. Life as a player can get quite stressful when things are not going well. The Valley is full of remembrances for him and so a garden of remembrance is something that he sets great store by as he sees people visit it day by day.

I think chaplains are really quite important to have around and I particularly think that when I see that garden of remembrance up there. That place in this stadium is quite important to me. I get quite moved when I see some of the people who go there. Sometimes it is quite young people and even children who are there scattering ashes and remembering people they love. I think it is a mark of the affection people have for the club that they want to do this. And it doesn't end there. They return at anniversary time and lay flowers. They may have moved on in life but they are still remembering. I think it is brilliant that the club and the chaplains offer this service.

In an age when professional football has become big business, to retain the personal touch is something that needs working at. As we have seen elsewhere in this book, the place of pastoral care in communities like this has real importance; supporters appreciate it because they are left feeling like real human beings with real human feelings and not simply as somebody else's investment. Place means people. For Colin Powell, preparing a pitch week by week, that is most important.

> I think that it is just great that I still enjoy getting up in the morning and coming to work, and I know so many people for whom that is simply not true. I think I have always felt that way about this place. I have a great affection for it whenever I think of it. It's a nice place to play football but I think what is even more important to me is that I have met so many nice people here in my time.

For Wendy Perfect, meeting supporters on a day-to-day basis leads her to conclude pretty much the same. It is a lifelong affection that many describe to her, for a place and the people that they remember as part of it.

> Because the football club plays such an important part in people's lives, this stadium and the garden are important as well and I know that because so many have asked me about what might happen to it in the event of re-development. I know the club will be sensitive to those feelings because it is the kind of club that takes care of details like that. Places are important and this one plays a part in completing the cycle of life. There are people who have been coming here since they were little kids and continued through their adult life into old age. They are the ones who sing 'I'm Charlton 'til I die' and they are. This place and that garden are a point of connection even when you have passed on.

So, when people continue to tell me that they are not particularly religious, I have another one of those smiles and wonder. They know the importance of what it means to have a home that is their own, a place of gathering to witness joy and disappointment. They know the importance of the past and the value in remembering the equivalent of their own communion of saints.

They know the place where they want to rest the memories of their heroes and sometimes to scatter the last remains of mortality that they knew and loved in life as friend or relative. They know the importance of the personal touch and how to make their own what has become special or even, dare I say, sacred space, all of which, at one level, sounds pretty religious to me.

12. You're not singing any more
An interview with Richard Rufus

MATT BAKER
Charlton Athletic

'And now the award for the greatest ever defender in the history of Charlton Athletic, voted by you the supporters, in this our centenary year, goes to . . . Richard Rufus.'

Charlton Athletic was founded as a football club in 1905 and so celebrated its centenary season in 2004–05. As part of these celebrations fans voted for their greatest ever Charlton game, greatest ever team and greatest individual players. As the tannoy announcement quoted above indicates, Richard received the honour of greatest ever defender. Such an award was no doubt fitting testimony for the player who made some 323 senior appearances and scored 13 goals. He was fearless and perfectly timed in the tackle, showed considerable pace and will always be remembered for scoring his first and most important goal in the Play-Off Final at Wembley in 1998. He was also three times voted the fans' player of the year, captained England at under-21 level and was working his way into contention for a first-team England place when a knee injury ended his career in 2004.

From my perspective as chaplain, it has been a privilege and a pleasure to get to know Richard not just as a player but as a friend. As a top Premiership defender, Richard became a Christian in 1998 and this chapter is taken from an interview with him about football and his faith, conducted on 4 November 2005.

How did you become a professional footballer?

Like many kids I spent a lot of my time playing football in the back garden and in the school playground. I really liked it, and when I was about eleven years of age I was invited to play for a Sunday football club. I was spotted playing for my Sunday club, London Boys (now Samuel Montagu), and invited for a trial at Arsenal when I was 12. I was quite excited about this as Arsenal was a world-known football club. I remember that game like it was yesterday, though I can't remember who we played against. We won something like 5–0 or 5–1 and thought I did quite well. However, the manager said they weren't interested in me and I was quite disappointed.

From there I was invited to train at Millwall, which was OK but I never really settled, so left of my own accord even though they wanted me to stay. A few weeks later a scout from Charlton spotted me playing for my district, Lewisham and Blackheath, and invited me down to Charlton. The first day I went down to Charlton I just knew it was for me. Charlton was a family-orientated football club and I knew a few people who I used to go to school with. At the age of 14 I signed schoolboy forms, which committed me to Charlton until I was 16.

When I turned 16 I had a meeting at Charlton; they said they liked the way I played, the way I had been performing and carrying myself, and I signed apprenticeship forms.

That was before the academy was set up, wasn't it?

Yes it was, I was an apprentice for two years and had to learn my trade. I had to watch my diet, train more or less every day, go to college once a week and do several apprenticeship chores like cleaning the pros' boots and vacuuming the training ground floor! It was a whole new culture to me, quite hard work, but I stuck at it because I wanted to be a professional footballer by the time I was 18.

So that was for two years until you were 18?

That's right and in those years I was playing against other apprentice teams throughout the country, and, as I improved, by the time I was 17 I was playing regularly in the reserves.

Did you get into the first team at all at that time?

No, not at that age. I had to be patient and bide my time and just work my way up, proving myself strong in the reserves.

When I was 18, about six of us were offered professional contracts. The day I signed professional forms it was the best thing that had ever happened to me. All I ever wanted was to be a professional footballer, and now I was getting the chance. But I also knew that the hard work had only just started; I knew that for me to progress now I needed to work my way from the bottom of the ladder upwards.

After my second year of playing in the reserves I got my break in the first team, when I was 19. There was an away game at Derby, and Curbs came to me and told me he was putting me down as sub. I remember sitting on the bench during that game, excited and nervous, wondering if I was physically and mentally strong enough for this – the big crowd, the stadium, all the supporters – it was completely different from playing reserve football. Anyhow, with 20 minutes left, I came on. I enjoyed every moment of it and after the game I thought, 'Yes, this is what I want every single week.' I think the result was 2–2 and I remember playing against Marco Gabbiadini.

The following week I made my full debut, away against Sunderland, and after being nervous for the first five minutes I settled down and really enjoyed it. From that point on I was a first-team regular and never looked back.[1]

After you got in the first team, were you still on this two-year contract?

After I got into the first team I think we negotiated a new contract. This was a much better contract, giving me a lot more money than I had been on previously.

So what was life like for you now with a lot more money, a regular first-team place and a good contract?

It was great really. Unlike being an apprentice, I was now in at 10.00, rather than 8.30. I trained for two to three hours and most of the time I was finished by about 12.30 or 1.00 compared to 4.30. Now I was in the position where I could go out and have nice holidays and buy most things I wanted. But this also meant a lot more temptation as I had a lot of time on my hands.

So how did you spend your time then?

I spent a lot of time going round my friends' houses, listening to music, mixing on record decks, playing Playstations and clubbing it.

Did you spend much time clubbing and drinking?

Yes, all the time – Saturday night, Sunday as well. Looking back now I don't know how I got away with it, because I went out so much I don't know how my football never suffered on the pitch. Every time there was an opportunity to socialize with the players, I was always among the first there. Because I was young and fit I was able to train the next day and could maintain my fitness.

So, from how you describe it, life was going very well. You were doing something you loved, earning well and playing week in, week out. At what point in all this, and indeed why, with everything going so well, did you get interested in Christianity?

Well, I started to realize that there are only so many clubs you can go to, only so many clothes you can buy, cars you can drive and holidays that you can go on. I actually felt frustrated, even though I'd experienced quite a lot of things at that age that most people would die for. Yet I felt, with all that, I was still a bit empty inside, I felt that there was still something missing in my life. Don't get me wrong, it was great having that lifestyle and playing football, but something inside was saying, 'There must be more to life than all of this.' So, I started talking to my aunt and uncle who are Christians, and asking them certain questions.

You didn't feel satisfied – is that what you're saying?

That's the bottom line; I never felt quite satisfied and contented with what I was doing as I still felt an emptiness that football or money could not fill. Also, I became more conscious and therefore convicted about the lifestyle that I was living.

No one came and said this to you; you just felt that something wasn't quite right?

That's right, something just wasn't quite right. I would also bump into people who said they wanted to be like me, they wanted to be a professional footballer, to live the lifestyle that I was living. Some people were worshipping me and yet I just felt like a normal person. I knew I'd been blessed to play football, which gave me some sort of celebrity status, but strip all that away and I'm just a normal person. I just didn't like that type of attention. I felt discontented about my lifestyle and there was something inside of me trying to pull me away from all of that.

So what did you do then?

Over a period of about twelve months I was searching, asking questions of my aunt and uncle and myself. I thought about Christianity, Islam and the Hindu religion, and was asking a number of questions: 'Why are we here as human beings?' 'What is our purpose, is it just to get drunk and have a good time?' 'If there is a God, am I living the way He wants me to?' 'Is there a heaven and hell?' 'What is all this about Jesus dying for my sins?' While searching I was reflecting on what had happened in my life. I wasn't really religious, but I was subconsciously praying to God. I prayed things like, 'OK, Lord, if there is a God please let me be a footballer by the time I'm 18 years of age,' and I was. Then, 'Let me play for England under 21s' and I found myself captaining England under 21s. So everything that I subconsciously prayed for, even though I wasn't a Christian, was happening.

Reflecting on this, I felt even more guilty; the Lord had blessed me in all this but I hadn't given anything back. In November 1998 it was more or less the culmination point. We had been promoted to the Premiership and yet I still wasn't contented in life. After all my thinking I said to my aunt, 'OK, I believe Christianity is the one, but I'll come and see you in thirty to forty years time; I'll have a good time first and then I'll give my life to Jesus.' Even though I was not contented in life I still couldn't let go of the lifestyle I had. But deep down that didn't feel right. I'd decided that Jesus was the way, the truth and the life, as it says in the Bible,[2] so I prayed a prayer asking him to forgive my sins and immediately committing my life to him. As soon as I prayed this, I felt a peace; it's hard to describe, but deep down I knew I had made the right decision.

How did people respond to you within football when you told them you'd become a Christian?

Some people only gave me three months and said I'd be back to how I was before. The players couldn't believe it: 'Christian, Richard, tough tackling, centre-back? There's just no way.' A few people thought my game was going to change physically.

Did it change physically?

No. I remember playing against a certain centre-forward, whom I won't name, and I tackled him quite hard. We both got up off the ground, at The Valley, and he said, 'I thought you were supposed to be a Christian.' I couldn't believe it and said, 'You're mistaken if you think that's going to stop me from tackling hard.'

How did your own team mates respond to you away from the matches?

Many people took me seriously. Over time quite a few came up to me and asked me to explain more about my faith and how it affected my life now and eternally. Some approached me privately to ask me to pray for them when they were going through problems. There was also quite a lot of leg-pulling like, 'Richard, what happened to the dinosaurs?' or 'How did everyone fit into Noah's ark?' But generally they respected me, I think.

You mentioned that you were just as hard physically on the pitch, but did your faith change the way you behaved in games?

Yes, it wasn't overnight, but over the months that followed I started to change. I might lose my temper occasionally, or swear, but I just prayed to overcome this. The last thing I wanted to do as a Christian was to set a bad example; I didn't want to let down my Lord, or other people, and I knew that some people were looking to me as a role model. With the Lord's help I tried to live a life that was consistent with the Bible, both on and off the pitch, whether I was playing or training.

I know that in the year after you became a Christian you had some difficult times. How did your faith help you then?

My faith was really stretched in the first 12 months. I knew as a Christian I should tithe, give 10 per cent of my wages, to my church. On the day I gave my first tithe, my car got broken into. Then, during that first season after I became a Christian, I broke my wrist in the January. Shortly after this I injured my leg, which kept me out for a few weeks; then I broke my hand in the March. In April, against Leeds, I was unfairly sent off for allegedly stamping on a player. Fortunately this was subsequently overturned on appeal by the FA who saw that I was completely innocent of any offence. Then, in the last week of the season, I twisted my ankle and injured my ligaments and was on crutches for about eight weeks. On top of all this, as a team we got relegated back to Division One. Four injuries, an unfair sending-off, my car broken into and relegation – all in the first year!

All of this really tested my faith because before I became a Christian I never had any of these problems. Now all of a sudden, when I became a Christian, everything seemed to be going wrong. I found this all difficult to cope with, but got the support of more mature Christians who explained that it was quite normal to go through this sort of testing some time in your life. I still found this difficult to take, but I decided to persevere and be faithful to God and not revert back to my old way of living.

I kept going and over the next 18 months everything more or less turned around. I felt I'd been put to the test; I could have given up on Christianity, but, trusting in God, he pulled me through it.

My football came on in leaps and bounds, and in the next season I got the Player of the Year award. I also scored six goals in the season, which I think is the most a centre-back has ever scored for Charlton in one season. On top of that, we got promoted back into the Premiership and in the following season we stayed up, and I again got voted Player of the Year. Because I was playing well, I was also given an improved contract.

These couple of years taught me a lot about being faithful to God and persevering during the difficult times, and also a lot about his favour to me.

In August 2001 you damaged your cruciate ligaments in your right knee, which kept you out of the game for eight months. A lot of players might get quite down at a time like that and it could have meant the end of your career. How did being a Christian help you through that?

When I got injured I found a lot of people tried to challenge my faith, particularly as I was out for so long. They questioned me as to why I was going through these things and even suggested I had done something to offend God, so maybe he was taking me out of football. I had a battle to answer those sort of questions, but it got to a point where I decided I didn't need to justify myself to anyone. My view was that people do get injured and being a Christian doesn't make you a super being that's immune from injury.

I found that God was good to me during those eight months and gave me a great sense of peace. Many players can't cope at such times and may turn to drink or to gambling. Some can't even go to the first-team game on a Saturday to watch their own team mates because it hurts them so much. Through prayer and my relationship with God I had a peace, and still felt able to go and watch the games. I must admit it got a little bit lonely training on my own in the gym, but I persevered and my faith in God helped me through. I continued going to church and had several people praying for me.

I also believe that God performed a miracle in healing my knee. When the injury was originally diagnosed, the doctor said I had actually snapped and ruptured my ligaments. I saw another doctor who said the same thing. I had a few people in the church pray for me and when I went to see a doctor for the third time I was told the ligaments had not been snapped or ruptured, but that I had just stretched them, so it wasn't as bad as they first imagined. The doctor said that they had made a mistake previously, but I couldn't understand how different doctors, without conferring, had made the same mistake. I put it down to prayer and that God had done a miracle. That encouraged me that everything was going to be OK. My first game back was against Tottenham. After being initially apprehensive, I thought I played OK, made a few hard tackles and my knee was fine. Ever since then this knee has been fine, and I put that down to God's healing.

Tell me about the injury that finished your career then. You came through one major injury and found God's peace and healing, continued playing for about a year and then what happened?

I came back from the cruciate injury in March and played the rest of that season. The next season I played from August to February, and that was when I injured my other knee.

How did it happen?

I remember it like it was yesterday. We were training; I went to chip the ball with my left leg and miss-kicked it, so I scuffed the ball and my leg hyper extended. I remember it looked quite funny, as some players were laughing, but when I tried to carry on it was sore so I had to stop training. I was sent for a scan that afternoon, but at first I never thought anything of it. I was told to rest for a couple of weeks before resuming training and playing. But it just wasn't the same when I started back; it didn't feel right when I was playing. I was taking anti-inflammatory tablets, icing it, laying off the weights and hoping it would just get better each day.

The turning point came in a home game against Leeds, which we lost heavily, 6–1. I don't really think I should have played that game. I was marking Alan Smith but I noticed that when he turned I just couldn't turn as sharply and as quickly as normal; it was like I was playing with a handicap and I couldn't turn and tackle properly. After this I saw the doctor and he diagnosed an osteochondral defect, which means that there's a hole in the bone. Depending on where this is, some players are able to play on for a few years. But for me it was serious because it was in the place where my knee bends, the joint itself. It's a bit like a pothole in the road, but in this case it's in my knee. This all made sense when I thought about why I couldn't turn properly; sometimes when I turned or squatted or tried to get up from the ground my knee would just give way.

In the weeks after the Leeds game I did play a couple more games. I knew then that I needed an operation, but it was near the end of the season, we were short of defenders, so I agreed to carry on playing. As I remember, in those weeks I was hardly training so that my knee would be OK for the games. Of course, this meant that I started to lose my general fitness and found it hard to last the 90 minutes. My last game was against Liverpool, even though there were a few games left before the end of the season, I just couldn't carry on physically, my knee couldn't take it any more. It was about then that I had the operation.

What happened after the operation?

I thought it was a straightforward operation and the doctor said I'd be back in action in three months. That was fine; all it meant was that I'd miss the first month of the following season. But as it turned out the process was much longer than that. Things were still not right when I started training again, but I thought it would be all right eventually, that I just had to go through the pain barrier. I got back to playing in the reserves, but then in the fourth game I played, against Arsenal, my leg hyper extended again. This led to my second operation in six months.

Again, I felt that my faith helped me through this time. At this point I didn't think about retiring at all, I had my spirits quite high and people were praying for me in the church.

However, as we came into November I began to get more frustrated as my knee still didn't feel right even though I was training, and then it broke down again. I had seen so many different specialists by then that we decided to go to see Dr Steadman, a world-renowned knee specialist in America. So I visited Dr Steadman in February the following year and had my third operation. After this I was the most confident I had been in eight months, and I was able to get out running and doing light weights without any pain.

But then, about two to three months after this operation, I started to feel the pain again. It was at this point I started to wonder whether this was the end of the road. I'd had three operations in less than twelve months, seen the top specialist in the world, and my knee still wasn't right. I went back to America to see Dr Steadman in May for a second consultation, but there was nothing really he could do. There was a new and untried method but it was still being experimented with on horses! Even trying this it would be a two-year procedure with no guarantees at the end of it. We'd really reached the end of the road.

So how did you cope with that as a Christian? With the previous injury you had a sense of God's peace and that he still wanted you to play; now with this injury you felt it was time to quit. Was your faith challenged by this?

Yes, my faith was challenged. I wondered whether it was down to my faith: had I prayed enough, had I fasted enough? It was quite hard and quite challenging, but I started to think about a verse in Ecclesiastes: 'There is a time for everything, and a season for every activity under heaven' (3.1). As I prayed and pondered this, I started to think that maybe my time as a footballer was over; maybe the Lord was leading me on to other things. As I started to think about retirement now, I still felt that same sense of peace and contentment and that he was going to lead me into something new.

I had really enjoyed playing football, but I thought that if the Lord was leading me into something else then maybe this would bring me even greater joy.

It's interesting to look back with hindsight on that time, but it makes more sense now. Being injured for nearly a year and a half, I can see how the Lord was building the foundations of what I am doing now.

How do you mean?

Well, it was a transitional period. I wasn't suddenly out of the game; it was a year and a half, so I felt like the Lord cushioned the blow.

But what do you mean by 'building the foundations of what you are doing now'?

Well, the things that I'm doing now I started to do when I was injured. If I hadn't put things into place then, I don't know what I would be doing now.

What things are they and why did you put them in place at this time?

I had a vision of what I would be doing. I remember I woke up one morning and told my wife that I'd had a dream about what I would be doing. I was still playing football at the time, but I had this dream about a month before I got injured.

So, you had a dream about your future?

Sort of. I didn't know I was going to retire, but yes, I had a dream about sorting out my financial investments and preparing for the future. Initially I put the dream to one side; I was still playing football and thought I had another seven years ahead of me. Even when I got injured a month later I still kept the dream to one side in my mind. But when I'd been injured for about four or five months, I started thinking about it again. I had a lot of time on my hands because I was injured, so I eventually went ahead with it, investing, putting money into property and setting up companies.

So you became obedient to that vision some five months on?

Yes, I realized that was why God had given me the dream. I felt the Lord opening my eyes to something I had never considered, and authorizing me to go ahead. As I did so I found quite a lot of success in the things I was setting up. But I still wasn't thinking about retiring; I thought the Lord wanted me to do it because I had so much time on my hands. I praise God now, looking back, and seeing how he had led me into those various activities.

So all this was very much driven by your faith?

Yes, Christianity for me is about a relationship and also getting to know the voice of the Lord. At the time I never knew that this injury was going to force my retirement, because I was only 28. But, at other times in my Christian life, I've had dreams and visions which have turned out to be true. I'm beginning to learn and hear the Lord's voice, so when I had this vision about investments and properties I believe it was the Lord speaking to me and directing me. That's why I say my faith is all about a relationship and getting to know his voice.

How have you spent your time since you retired from the game two years ago now?

Well, to start with I've stayed obedient to the vision, and for the first year I was very busy with the properties and the companies I was setting up. I also started a degree a few years ago in biblical studies, so I have been continuing with this.

As well as this, of course, I am still involved in my church. I like to visit churches and other places to talk about my faith, both what it meant to me when I was playing football and what it means to me now. I keep stressing that while football was great, it's not the be all and end all in life. I don't agree with other retired footballers who say that there's no greater buzz in life apart from football.

Since I've retired there have been times when I have really missed playing football. Of course, this is natural as I had played football all my life since leaving school, but my faith in God has given me strength.

So do you think your future lies in the Church or some form of Christian work?

Oh yes, without a shadow of a doubt. Even with the properties I have been involved with I don't have as much passion in that as I have for my involvement in the Church and sharing the gospel with others. I'd say my passion for that is similar, even greater, than what I had for football.

Can you see yourself in pastoral ministry perhaps?

Maybe so, but it's still early days for me; I've only just come out of one career. I just want to be faithful to what the Lord has given me and what he wants me to do in the next season of my life.

Do you feel because of what you've been through, you have something to say to young players in preparing them for their future?

Yes, as I already do speak to young people about the ups and downs of being a professional footballer and my experience. I guess I've seen quite a lot in the last 12 years. One thing I suppose I never had was someone telling me what it would be like when I finished my career, and that there is life after football.

There's a lot of pressure within football to succeed. How would you define success, and what it means in your life for now and the future?

I would define success from a Christian perspective, as fulfilling what God has called you to be. I believe to a certain degree I was successful, because part of my purpose in life was to be a footballer. We all have different roles, we all have different seasons, and I believe as long as you are fulfilling the purpose that God has called you to for that season you are successful. God created me to play football for a certain time in my life, and I believe I made the grade in what he wanted – that's success. If he takes me out of football and he wants to make me a doctor, for example, as long as I'm a good doctor in that field I'm successful.

In terms of my life now, I still think I'm in a transitional stage. However, God has the last word and I guess I won't really know whether my life has really been a success until I meet him in heaven. When I hear him say, 'Well done my good and faithful servant', then I'll know that it has been a success.

13. What's the SCORE?

RAY DUPERE
Watford and SCORE

You are almost at the end of a book about chaplaincy in the world of association football, but you will not get far in this section without detecting something unmistakeably un-English or even un-British about the author; and you would be right. I am an American who has long been in love with the beautiful game.

If you're still with me at this point I am really glad and maybe I can now offer some kind of explanation for why I am here, how I came to fall in love in this way, and what the heck I am doing this side of the pond operating as chaplain to Watford Football Club and working for the sports charity SCORE. There is no explanation for why I'm an American; I had no control over that. I'm an American because I was born in America. Put very simply, it would be too hard for me to write this chapter without first admitting to who I really am, because who I am has emerged through the experience of life I have acquired, and a lot of that has been formed in the United States. For me it's simply easier to write out of my own personal real-life context, rather than an artificial one. So, that's the confession. Now I want to tell you how it all began for me.

My first exposure to soccer (OK, make some allowance for me, I am an American) did not occur until I was about 18 years old, in September of 1965. At the time, I was just beginning my first year as a cadet at the US Military Academy in West Point, New York. In those days all cadets were required to participate in organized sports during each of the seasons of autumn, winter and spring. As a first-year cadet, I was not really given the option of what sport I wanted to play; I was simply assigned to the D-3 (Company D, 3rd Regiment) soccer team. As the saying goes, I remember that first day like it was yesterday.

It was a beautiful scene, on a warm, hazy day, down along the banks of the Hudson River. There were probably about eighteen of us gathered together for our team, with twenty-four other teams forming up on about a dozen soccer fields. The captain of the team (who was one of the fourth-year students) started calling out our names, and checking them off on a clipboard. Then he asked if anyone had ever played soccer before; out of the group, maybe two or three had played. After asking what positions people had played, he asked who thought they might be fast, and so on. And then came the moment that truly did, for ever, change my answer to the question, 'What's your favourite sport?' He asked if anyone might want to be the goalkeeper. In a split second, all kinds of thoughts went through my head.

First was the fact that I had a choice to make. One little piece of my destiny at West Point was in my hands. Then, too, was the realization that the position of goalkeeper might be something that I could do. I had grown up playing baseball, and for most of my playing days I played the position of catcher, which is a bit like a wicketkeeper in cricket. So I thought that if I could play catcher, I might be able to play goalkeeper as well. In addition to that, it also occurred to me that if I did play in the goal, then at least I wouldn't end up sitting on the dreaded bench the whole season. So, I raised my hand and said that I'd be willing to try my hand in the goal.

I don't remember if I was automatically given the job, or if there was some kind of trial, but in the end I became the starting goalkeeper for the D-3 soccer team, and, as it turned out, I was actually quite good. In fact, our team went on to be one of the best teams in the whole corps of cadets. We ended up losing out on going to the championship finals by an own goal. I played goalkeeper for three more years after that, and, through it all, I came to love 'the beautiful game'. So much so that years later, when I was in seminary in Dallas, Texas, I never went to a single Dallas Cowboys (American) football game. But I did go to two or three professional soccer games that were played during my time there.

I tell that story for two reasons. First is to say that I love soccer. I love it more than any American sport that I may have played or watched while I was growing up. And, second, it's because of my love of soccer that I ended up coming to live in England to work with SCORE. I truly do doubt that I would have ever moved here, or even thought about moving here, if it hadn't been for that September day in 1965 when I was first infected with the soccer bug.

What's the SCORE?

So what is this organization called SCORE that I have now come to work for? Well, let's start with the name. What do the letters S-C-O-R-E stand for? Simply put, they stand for 'Sports Chaplaincy Offering Resources and Encouragement'. It goes without saying that the name was probably picked before the meaning was then decided upon. But even so, it does explain what we do. Sports chaplains exist to provide pastoral care and encouragement to people who work and play in professional sports in England. In addition, SCORE also exists to provide resources and encouragement to sports chaplains. And since there is no other similar organization, you could say we are *the* sports chaplains' network in the United Kingdom.

In a previous chapter of this book you will have read that SCORE was officially founded in 1991 by John Boyers, while he was still the chaplain at Watford Football Club. Back then, football was the only sport with which SCORE and sports chaplaincy in England were really involved. As you will see later, that has since changed quite significantly; but with football being the only sport, SCORE seemed like a name that made perfect sense. However, with expansion into other sports, especially sports where the concept of a 'score' was not as relevant, the suggestion of a change in our name has been discussed.

Why a sports chaplains' network?

To those of us who work full time (or even part time) for SCORE, and for a lot of the chaplains in our network, the existence of SCORE makes perfect sense. However, even though it might make sense to us, it may not make sense to others, so let me expound for a while on why a sports chaplains network is a worthwhile thing.

The existence of our network gives us a chance to . . . well . . . network. This is primarily accomplished through the 'fraternals' and the annual sports chaplains' conference. Our fraternals are smaller regional get-togethers that take place a couple of times a year, usually in late winter or early spring, and then again in early summer. Our annual conference is usually held in early October, and for quite a few years now it has been held at the Lilleshall National Sports Centre near Telford. The conference is usually spread over three days, from lunch on a Tuesday through to lunch on a Thursday, with a typical schedule including a time of Bible teaching each day, as well as numerous sessions devoted to various aspects of professional sports or to sports-related ministry.

In the past we've had guest speakers who have included chief executive officers and managers from Premier League, Football League and non-League clubs. We've had speakers from the Football Association (the FA), the League Managers' Association (LMA), the Professional Footballers' Association (PFA), and representatives from the Premier League and the Football League. We've had current and former club managers, coaches and players. In addition, we also have sessions where we provide specific teaching or training, or just the sharing of practical suggestions on different aspects of sports ministry or life in sports. Throughout the three days we intersperse our group sessions with time for simple interaction or networking or fellowship.

In our most recent conference, there were a total of just over sixty persons in attendance, with the majority of these being either former chaplains, current chaplains or prospective chaplains. Though there is always room for improvement, the majority of the feedback received indicates that those who attended the conference appreciated the opportunity to get away together.

While it seems to me that the chaplains at conference have a common love of sport as a unifying factor, those who participate at conference all start with a love for God based on God's love for us. Within the greater context of that love of God we find our common love of sports, and it is out of this that we find ourselves 'Serving Sport through Chaplaincy'. This is SCORE's motto. So it follows, then, that in serving God through sport, we bring a dimension of friendship to a world of competition that can sometimes be lacking. Chaplains at conference find this in the support and encouragement they can give each other, even in such a short time together. Our chaplains always seem to enjoy the conference. The friendship fostered among fellow sports chaplains is so positive it tends to be the overarching feature and nearly always compensates for any shortcomings that might appear in the conference programme itself.

John Boyers, in Chapter 2, writes about the formative years of chaplaincy and the work done at Watford Football Club, which led to the eventual establishment of chaplaincy as an important ingredient of club life. I am convinced that without something like SCORE, sports chaplaincy as it is practised today in the UK probably wouldn't exist – or at least it wouldn't be as advanced as we see it now.

Offering resources and encouragement?

SCORE provides written resources and personal advice, counsel and encouragement to its constituent chaplains, and they in turn provide encouragement and some resources to their clubs. So what are some of the resources that SCORE provides?

For one thing, we can provide clubs and potential chaplains with our code of practice, so they know what to expect should the club decide to utilize a chaplain, or the prospective candidate actually get to serve as a chaplain. Then, too, we can provide chaplains with a variety of materials. For example, club and community carol services are not uncommon these days. We also have sample services for the scattering of ashes following a funeral. Not every club allows for all of these activities; but enough clubs do so provide for such occasions that it makes sense for us to be prepared in this way. So we provide materials as needed and when called upon. With the SCORE network now at over a hundred and fifty chaplains spread throughout the UK, some chaplain somewhere is going to have a question about something that might well have been dealt with by another chaplain in another part of the country. This happens on a fairly regular basis. Through the expertise of our full-time staff, we seek to help any individual chaplain with any need that they might have. Whatever their question, it falls upon us either to provide the answer or to find the answer if we can't provide it outright. Here's a case in point. In the autumn of 2005, Stuart Wood, who was our newest chaplain at the time, having been recently appointed to Cambridge United Football Club, sent us an email with a question about performing weddings and blessings at the Abbey Stadium in Cambridge. He wanted to know if any of our other SCORE chaplains had a policy on such requests at their sports clubs. Did any of them have any experience or guidelines that they could share with him? Since about 75 per cent of our chaplains have overcome their fear of the Internet, I simply forwarded his email on to our online network. All together, he received responses from about a dozen chaplains; and from what I could tell, obtained enough information to get him started towards a solution at Cambridge United.

Other examples of resources that SCORE can provide include academy training outlines, sample job descriptions, generic home match day programme pieces, and so on. Much of our materials were developed by John Boyers during his formative years at Watford Football Club, and often they came out of enquiries from our chaplains, similar to the one with Cambridge United's chaplain described above. However, sometimes the resources come directly from our chaplains themselves; the sample job description is a good instance. At our regional fraternals, we often give each of the chaplains in attendance the opportunity to share what might be happening at their respective clubs. At one such fraternal in South Yorkshire, the host chaplain mentioned that he had been working with his club's human resources director on a job description for his role as chaplain. The other chaplains asked if they could have a look at it. So he went off and got some copies made; and afterwards we all looked it over and had a chat about the bullet points in the job description, and about the value of developing a job description for each of our different clubs.

As it turned out, later that same month, one of our recently appointed chaplains called asking if we had a sample job description that he could use. He said that one of the officers at his club had asked him what exactly a chaplain did, and so the question of a job description had arisen. We emailed him a copy of the job description previously mentioned, and he was then able to adapt it to his club setting and use it to answer the question about what a chaplain does.

However, describing what we do doesn't always clarify what a chaplain is meant to be (and Chapter 1 of this book poses just that question, 'Who are you?'). It's not an uncommon or unreasonable question for any chaplain to face. Drawing up a job description can go some way towards defining what a chaplain thinks he or she is about. It would usually be standard practice for people who are employed by a club to make such a definition of their work practice. By seeking to develop a job description within our various club settings, it can help to bridge the gap between a chaplain feeling as though they are on the outside looking in, and feeling an integral part of the whole club structure.

So that gives some idea of how SCORE provides resources, but what about encouragement? How is that provided? It is provided in a number of different ways. Just having the opportunity to be with other like-minded chaplains at the fraternals and our annual conference is a form of encouragement, but it goes beyond that.

Let me illustrate my point by referring to something that came out of our most recent conference. Of the sixty or so persons attending the last conference at Lilleshall, only two were women. This says quite a lot about the current gender make-up of chaplaincy right across the sporting world. At the present time in the UK its composition is overwhelmingly male. This poses an important challenge for all of us in chaplaincy generally and at SCORE in particular. I am glad to say that it is one that we have already begun to address. Mary Vickers, an ordained Anglican, was one of the two. Mary was recently appointed as SCORE's Co-ordinator of Chaplaincy for Women in Sport. The other, Carolyn Skinner, a young pastor from the London area, is interested in becoming one of our volunteer chaplains in the future. After the conference, Mary sent me an email in which she says:

I was really pleasantly surprised about how well integrated into the conference both Carolyn and I found ourselves. As a female Church of England minister, I'm well used to being in a male-dominated situation at conferences and meetings over the last 20 years; and, although I've often been the only woman in smaller groupings, I've rarely been to a conference where the numbers were so large and thus the balance was so weighted towards men. I was slightly wary before I came, but both Carolyn and I said to each other on Wednesday evening that it had been a good experience and there'd been very, very few comments and jibes about women, and we both really appreciated that. I do know that there were people there who don't necessarily approve theologically of women clergy/pastors/ministers but all the ones I was aware of treated me with respect, which was really appreciated, and I hope that I was as sensitive back to them. Maybe this is a sad reflection in some parts of the church where this is not always the case (trust me, it isn't always like it was at SCORE!!) but I wanted to say how good it was at Lilleshall these past few days.

I checked with Carolyn, and she agreed that Mary's words were an accurate reflection of how she felt as well. I was very encouraged that Mary and Carolyn felt so accepted. Too often those of us who work in sports ministry (and here I am not just referring to SCORE, but to other ministries as well) find ourselves misunderstood by the wider Church. And, as Mary alluded, women in ministry often feel misunderstood in the wider Church as well. SCORE has a golden opportunity in Mary's appointment and the doors it might open up to establish a model of chaplaincy support that takes women seriously in chaplaincy as in sport. It is all very well for us to declare that God is love and that we serve God through the vehicle of chaplaincy, but if that model of chaplaincy is one in which women experience misunderstanding and non-acceptance, we pay it little more than lip service. The existence of SCORE isn't just a nice option, it is essential to our individual health and well-being as sports chaplains, and it needs to take a lead in a world where women often feel (and are) undervalued and overlooked.

Ready for the future?

Our ultimate goal is for every professional football club, rugby league and rugby union club, and every county cricket club, etc., to have an officially designated club chaplain. However, we don't want chaplains just to be window dressing. We want real chaplains on the ground in their sports clubs providing a professional ministry of caring for and serving sports people as they deal with the real problems of life. In addition, we want every chaplain and sports chaplaincy as a concept to be acknowledged as a vital part of every club and its purposes. We want professional sports organizations to see us as professionals too. We have unique gifts and abilities that we can bring to bear within a club to make it a better place because of our having been there. Let me give you one example of what I mean.

About thirty years ago, the whole field of crisis intervention began to be more formally developed in the United States. Eventually, an organization called the International Critical Incident Stress Foundation in Baltimore, Maryland, was founded. Today, especially due to the increased threat of terror since 9/11, their critical incident stress management (CISM) techniques are being taught and put into practice around the world.

In April of 2005, SCORE took its first steps in seeking to train its chaplains in critical incident or crisis response techniques. We did this by offering two one-day seminars to our chaplains at the Northampton Saints Rugby Union FC's Franklin's Gardens Stadium and at Barnsley Football Club's Oakwell Stadium. As the seminars were being taught, the discussion was never what to do *if* a terrorist incident should occur, but rather what to do *when* an incident occurred. The events that unfolded in London on 7 July 2005 held a particular poignancy for our organization when we heard the news that one of our prospective chaplains with a particular interest in motor sports was killed at Kings Cross station that day.

At SCORE we know that we have some specialized training to offer our chaplains that might one day make them more useful to their clubs in the event of what local authorities call a 'major incident'. This might be in response to a terrorist incident, but equally it might describe some other disaster such as occurred at the Bradford or Hillsborough football grounds. Of course, as with everyone else, we pray that day will never come. But if it does, we would hope to have the chaplains we support ready, and, through their efforts, we would also hope to have their clubs better equipped to respond should a critical incident occur at a sporting event. It's all part of our desire to see sports chaplains and sports chaplaincy become increasingly more professional; and in so doing, to see it become more recognized as having a legitimate place in the world of professional sports.

SCORE is a charity?

Because the primary focus of SCORE is to provide chaplaincy services to professional sports, people often think we must be rolling in money. If only that were the case! The reality is that SCORE tends to have a difficult time keeping on top of financial matters, even though we are a very frugal organization. The bulk of our time, especially when consulting or liaising with sports organizations, is offered without remuneration. SCORE accepts invitations to serve wherever we believe we can extend the work of God's Kingdom in the area of sport, irrespective of the likelihood of a direct financial contribution to SCORE.

Serving sport through chaplaincy is what it says. First and foremost, we seek to serve, not to be served. We do this by providing pastoral care, on a voluntary basis, to those who live and work in the world of professional sports. It is absolutely imperative that we approach all that we do with a servant's heart. The last thing we can afford to do, if we are to maintain our long-term credibility, would be regularly to go to the world of sport cap in hand. Consequently, SCORE is an officially recognized charity (UK Registered Charity Number 1005446), and is funded by donations from a wide range of sources. These include grants from denominational sources, various football bodies, and the horse-racing industry, as well as other grant-making bodies and trusts. The remaining funds come from individuals and churches, tax refunds and fundraising events, etc.

It costs over £115,000 a year, or £315 every day, to keep SCORE running. This is needed to cover stipends for our two full-time paid employees (based on the recommended denominational standard stipends), housing allowances, statutory insurance and pension contributions, travel costs, phones, stationery, publicity, office and conference costs. As with all charities, funding is a major issue, without which we cannot expand or even continue the current level of ministry that God has opened up to us.

SCORE and new horizons

Whatever else we get to do at SCORE, I hope that we go on trying to realize the potential that we have for chaplaincy. If we are going to grow we will need to do that, and it will happen most successfully by appreciating the greatest significance in some of the smallest things. Let me close this chapter with a story beyond the world of football that opened my eyes to this.

Soon after my arrival in England, back in October 2003, John Boyers and I went to an international sports ministry conference in Greece. The conference itself was quite an experience. It lasted for about a week, and included over 750 delegates from more than 175 different countries around the world. I'm quite sure that I will never be at another such event this side of heaven! However, that's not what this story is about. Rather it's about what happened after the conference when John and I spent three days in Athens before heading back to England.

While we were in Athens, the local Anglican priest arranged for us to pay a visit for about three hours to ATHOC, the 2004 Athens Olympic Organizing Committee headquarters. While there, we met with the person who had the daunting task of organizing everything that had anything to do with activities within the Olympic Village. Among all the other things this individual had to do, one responsibility was to co-ordinate religious activities within the Olympic Village. And as it turned out, at that time, not much in the way of plans had been made.

Up until our meeting, the sole concept of providing for the religious needs of the athletes was a plan to provide a room where a couple of 'religious officials' could hang out, in case any athletes wanted to come to the room to talk to them. Not only that, but these 'religious officials' were going to be absolutely forbidden to go anywhere else in the Olympic Village except for the religious activities room! This was apparently because ATHOC feared that a threatening, in-your-face style of ministry might otherwise be the result. However, as John began to share from his experience at the 2002 Commonwealth Games in Manchester, England, it was interesting to watch the officials in charge begin to loosen up as it became apparent that their concept of 'religious activities' was quite different from what had been done there. As the national director of SCORE, John had been picked to be the director of chaplaincy services for Manchester 2002. Under John's leadership, a chaplaincy team of over twenty-five ministers from various Christian denominations and other religious faith groups had ministered throughout the various venues, as well as in the Athletes' Village. So John brought a wealth of experience to the Athens meeting.

One of the things that we stressed was that the chaplains needed to have access to the athletes out in the Olympic Village, and not be confined to a little room somewhere. We pointed out that the whole concept of being a chaplain involves going to the people you minister to, rather than waiting for them to come to you. Especially since, in many cases, they simply cannot get away from their own responsibilities, but still want to have someone they can talk to. During some of this part of the discussions, I was able to draw on my military chaplaincy experience to clarify the point further. Anyway, by the time we were done, those concerned had come around to the point where SCORE was invited to help organize the chaplaincy services that took place within the Olympic Village.

Several positive outcomes emerged as a consequence of this initial meeting, with ATHOC appreciating our professional, caring and sensitive expression of chaplaincy. First, chaplains were not confined to a small room, but were given the freedom to go out into the Olympic Village to minister to the athletes; second, instead of just a couple of religious officials, there were well over fifty chaplains assigned to serve in the Athletes' Village; third, SCORE helped ATHOC determine what the mix of denomination etc. would probably be, and helped develop the procedures for choosing who was qualified to serve as a chaplain. To cap it all, John travelled to Athens to serve as the co-ordinator of the Protestant chaplaincy team for the

Olympic Village for both the 2004 Olympic and Paralympic Games.

What started as one man's response to an open door that God put before him at Watford Football Club back in the 1970s has expanded to become a concept and a ministry that is recognized and appreciated around the world. John Boyers can not have known where this ministry would lead, and the question we are left with at the end of this chapter is 'Where does it go now?' In the following chapter, Mary Vickers will look at how this question is being addressed through the insights of women in football specifically, and chaplaincy in the world of sport generally. Can it really be going nowhere? I don't think so.

14. Nowhere; you're always going nowhere

MARY VICKERS
SCORE

'Nowhere; you're always going nowhere' is one of the more merciless taunts from the terraces you might hear on a Saturday afternoon. It is nearly always directed to an opposition that is thought to be a bit above itself or one whose ambitions are clearly beyond their abilities. Reserved for the one-season-wonder team, the under-achiever or the self-important, the aim is to unsettle and bring the opposition down with a demoralized bump. As we have seen, much of football copies life, and this is no different. It happens everywhere, be it in school playgrounds, bars, workshops, factories, offices or other sports arenas around the land. Nobody likes to be going nowhere or thought to be going nowhere. Christians and others of major faith backgrounds often find themselves on the receiving end of this accusation. Sometimes they are called upon to explain themselves, or to justify their belief in God in the face of this or that situation. Sometimes it is the accusation of 'pie in the sky when you die', or the accusation that there is somehow something lacking in us because we believe in God – something I remember being thrown at me when I owned my faith for myself as an adult, as if it somehow insulted my intelligence and integrity because the Christian faith had become part of my life.

As a Christian minister, the challenge to respond to this kind of charge comes quite frequently, especially when one steps out of the church building or immediate church context into another arena. While within the confines of the church, we're in our 'proper' place and aren't seen as bothering anyone who doesn't want to be bothered by us; but once we step across the threshold, and begin to engage actively with the world around, people are not always sure what we're doing in the situation they find us. When we do that, there is the thought that we're engaged on a fruitless occupation at best, and that we'll achieve nothing and go nowhere. Or perhaps it is simply a misunderstood move?

Chaplaincy in any field is an extension of this engagement with the world outside the confines of the church. I firmly believe that where people are, there the Church should be; hence my involvement in chaplaincy in various contexts since my ministerial training. Although attending church and leading services is obviously important to me as a priest, I was once heard to say that 'I've always been happier outside the church than in it'! This is why I've often been involved in chaplaincy. Clergy used to be able to visit everyone in their parish or area on a regular basis, but as parishes, Methodist circuits and other local church areas have got larger and larger, this is now an impossibility for all but those who minister in the smallest communities. Also, in our mobile and busy society, many people don't get the chance to attend church regularly as a result of their work or family situation; and so, through offering chaplaincy, I and others like me are able to offer care and support with a spiritual dimension to those who want it, wherever they are, at work or at play or in a situation of particular need. Some people won't see a need for this, but chaplaincy is there for this – as St Augustine once said, 'There is a God-shaped hole in all of us.' Chaplaincy often feels like a waiting game, and much of the time one can feel as though no progress is being made. One female football club chaplain once coined the phrase 'creatively hanging around' to describe chaplaincy, adding that while doing it you sometimes 'feel like a lemon' but you still continue doing it. I've adopted a similar phrase – 'loitering with intent' – because, alongside periods of sometimes intense activity, chaplaincy includes a lot of simply being around, waiting to be made use of, and then enabling things to happen. Thus, the football chant 'nowhere; you're always going nowhere' could often be directed at many chaplains whether in sport or otherwise. As someone once said,

'If you don't know where you are going, you'll probably end up somewhere else'!

Whether or not the first women to play football knew where they were going, and where their actions might lead, will always remain an unanswered question. Football in the UK is still seen by many as a man's game, whether one is talking about players, officials or spectators. However, this is beginning to change, as is evidenced by the increase in women players, as well as women officials, administrators and coaches. There has also been an increase in female spectators in recent years, but whether this is to do merely with the attraction of the game itself (played by either men or by women) or whether it has come about as a result of the Taylor report is arguable. This report was commissioned after the Hillsborough disaster in 1989, where 96 fans were crushed to death, and called for a new image for football with all-seater stands, better facilities, and a 'family atmosphere' where women and children could be welcomed. The idea behind this last aspect is that women were seen as having an important role in 'civilizing' potentially volatile crowds, thus offsetting the aggression and violence of a predominantly male fan base. It attempted to herald a fresh start for UK football. However, women's involvement in football, whether as players or as fans, is not a new thing. There is, for instance, evidence that women were permitted free entrance to some professional club grounds in the late nineteenth century. This privilege ceased in 1885 after an Easter Monday game at Preston at which some two thousand women and girls were alleged to have been present.[1]

Men's football was officially recognized in 1863, with the first professional league established in 1888; but there is some debate as to when women first started playing football seriously. The first recorded organized game of women's football seems to have happened on 23 March 1895, when a representative match between northern and southern women's teams took place at Crouch End, London. Seven years later, the FA Council forbade its member teams from playing against 'lady teams' and, without official encouragement and support, women's football floundered until the First World War. This heralded a huge growth in the game as women took on jobs and responsibilities previously filled by men, and also began enjoying some traditional male pastimes alongside this. The new women's teams in wartime were based around factories and, as well as providing relief from work, often raised money for war charities. The most successful team was Dick Kerr's Ladies from Preston – Dick Kerr's being the munitions factory that the female players worked for. By the end of the war, the numbers of teams had increased across the country and they attracted huge crowds. On Boxing Day 1920, fifty-three thousand people were reported to have watched Dick Kerr's beat St Helen's Ladies 4–0 at Goodison Park, with an estimated further ten to fourteen thousand people locked outside.

By the 1920s, there were around a hundred and fifty teams, and women's football in England was attracting more interest and bigger crowds; in some cases bigger crowds than low-ranking men's matches, a situation the FA found difficult to accept. On 5 December 1921, the FA banned member clubs from allowing women to play on Football League grounds. Although other reasons were cited in addition, the true sentiment of the ban was probably found in the FA's statement that it was of the 'strong opinion that the game of football is quite unsuitable for females and should not be encouraged'.

This effectively ended the wartime boom in women's football in England. Women continued to play between the wars but there was no league structure and various players and officials who had coached or refereed women's football found themselves having to be careful of associating with women's football lest they fall foul of the FA themselves. Players became hard to attract, matches were infrequent and so became viewed by some as a bit of a joke. This remained the situation until a resurgence of interest in the women's game in the late 1960s. Many attribute this to the enthusiasm following England's triumph in the 1966 World Cup. Younger women began to see it as a serious sport and as one to which they should have more access. The Women's Football Association was founded in 1969, and this was followed in 1972, under pressure from UEFA, by the lifting of the FA ban on women playing on Football League grounds in England.

Since the early 1970s, there has been a gradual increase in

the numbers of women players in England. By 1989, there were 263 women's clubs and around 7,000 players; in 1990, 314 and 9,000 registered players; and the figure for 1992–93 was 450 with 12,000 registered players. Figures for the 1997–98 season show a total of 1,700 women's and girls' teams with 34,000 registered players.[2] In 2005, there were 131,500 girls and women registered and playing the game in over 9,600 affiliated teams throughout England, up 30 per cent in a year from 101,173 registered players in 2004.[3]

There are many parallels between the situation for women in football and women involved in other fields previously seen as traditional male preserves – including the ministry of the Church. The roles of men and women vary between different societies and communities. In each case, norms for what are acceptable activities for each gender are based on its cultural history, and the definition of most activities and groups will be influenced by ideological beliefs of what it means to be a 'woman' or a 'man', to be 'feminine' or 'masculine'. Ideas obviously develop and change over time, but such changes often demonstrate that some things are very deep-rooted in a society's collective psyche. Even in our contemporary and increasingly multicultural society, there are still some very strong and powerful messages about 'femininity', which have meant that it has been difficult for women to break into, and be taken seriously in, some of those sports defined as 'masculine'. The same could be said to be true of the Church, where the predominant view until the last century or so has been that its leadership is a 'male' preserve. In 1902, when the FA Council forbade men's teams from playing against women's teams, in addition to 'offending middle-class propriety' one of the reasons was that some in the medical profession felt that football would 'damage female reproductive organs'.[4] While I've never heard the latter reason given for not involving women in the leadership of the Church, I have heard things similar to the former implied on more than one occasion!

It was Dr Johnson in 1763 who said: 'A woman preaching is like a dog's walking on his hind legs. It is not done well; but you are surprised it is done at all.' I have been familiar with this quotation for a long time, but was surprised to see it quoted in altered form to apply to women's football. Other similarities between women in football and in the Church are highlighted by the comments of a Norwegian female referee who only in 1995 said, 'We have to be better than men if we want to referee at the same level as they do in men's games.'[5] Having heard many female ministers say the same, I can only hope that things are smoother for Lisa Rashid, who at the age of 18, is at level 4 of the referees' ladder and already ranked among the country's top 11 female referees. Also qualified as a coach in football, basketball and athletics, she says:

> I do get comments from supporters, players and managers. I think they're shocked to see me turn up because I'm a lady of colour and so young. I'm also a real 'girly girl' . . . I'm a female who loves doing her nails, adores shopping and takes time to put on her make-up . . . But I wouldn't be where I am today if I didn't know the rules of the game.[6]

What a wonderful collection of supposedly conflicting stereotypes combined in one person's experience!

Some of the pioneers of women's football had to be very careful about their actions off the field as well as on it, if they were not to fall foul of people's comments and opinions. There were obviously some successes in countering people's reactions – for instance, Lopez tells how at a celebratory dinner in 1937, when Dick Kerr's Ladies had convincingly beaten a Belgian team 5–1, a Preston MP said, 'he had heard how tough they were but now he could see for himself, that although they played a man's game, they hadn't lost any of their femininity!'[7] One of the instructions to players from Manchester Corinthians, another team of the same era, was that trousers mustn't be worn to away matches: 'We are called Corinthian Ladies and we will dress like ladies.'[8] Several other women's teams had similar rules about not wearing trousers when travelling with the team. Similarly, a number of the first women to be ordained deacon in the Church of England in 1987 avoided wearing their clerical collars with trousers to avoid the accusation that we were merely trying to be like men. When Frank Keating had written in the *Guardian* ten years earlier that football could be a 'lovely game for women. What they need to do now is redefine it in

feminine terms, not ape the men so much . . . so that it comple-
ments their nature rather than compromises it,'[9] he could well
have been talking about women clergy, who have had the task
of redefining what the Church's ministry might look like when
it is not solely male. 'Nowhere; you're always going nowhere'
is not a taunt that should be directed at women in football, or
indeed in any sport. Neither should it be directed at women in
church leadership. Hopefully, all can soon sing together, 'Somewhere; we're simply going somewhere.'

When chaplains are apparently busy 'going nowhere', they
are often simply learning how to get alongside, seeking to sit
where sportspeople sit, and speak the language that they speak.
This, though, is a delicate balance, and there are pitfalls to
avoid. Although each chaplain should understand the context
in which they minister, an overemphasis on identification with
those ministered among can lead to a diluting of the chaplain's
vocation and effectiveness. Many football club chaplains are
also fans of the game. My main sporting involvement outside of
chaplaincy is in athletics. Other chaplains work in other sports.
Although our knowledge of, and involvement in, various sports
and sporting disciplines can greatly help us in our chaplaincy,
we must always remember that it is the person we are talking
to who is the athlete and not us. A chaplain should not be a
sports fanatic living out their fantasy or sporting ambition by
way of their chaplaincy; neither should they be keeping such a
distance or maintaining a kind of aloofness, so as to give the
appearance of the 'vicar ambling around'. Chaplains who have
too few points of contact with those they serve among will be
able to give little.

This is why I believe that time spent 'loitering with intent' is
immensely useful within chaplaincy. Yes, it can be misunderstood, as it was on one occasion when I was a retail chaplain. I
had been talking to a shop assistant in a large department store,
and, having developed eyes in the back of my head, realized
that there were customers who wanted to ask questions. I made
a comment to the salesperson I was talking to, stepped aside,
allowing her to do her work, and occupied myself by looking
through the racks of rather expensive ladies' clothes that were
nearby. The customers obviously had complicated enquiries as

I was there for quite a while – until I was spoken to from behind by someone asking whether I had yet found what I was looking for. Conversation revealed that this was in fact a store detective; it transpired that I was suspected of loitering with intent for dishonest rather than honourable chaplaincy purposes!

However, this has not stopped me from engaging in this approach. I spent many hours riding the buses around the circular bus routes within the Olympic Village at Athens 2004. Sometimes I would begin conversations with people on the buses, and begin making relationships that way. At other times, I would just ride, mostly standing, but occasionally sitting on seats that faced outwards to the rest of the bus. Being the sport I am most familiar with, I also spent time just walking around the athletics track in the village – never interrupting anyone's training, but observing and being observed. On a number of occasions, people who'd seen from my shirt or my badge that I was a chaplain began a conversation themselves; at other times, I would be proactive and begin talking to someone by greeting them in a friendly and sensitive way, and in their own language if I could manage it. I know of several people who came to the Religious Services Centre purely because they'd seen chaplains around, and so knew we must be somewhere about. One can never fully know the value of time spent 'loitering with intent'.

I walked miles around York Racecourse in June 2005 when I was a chaplain during Royal Ascot at York, and spoke with many people. However, I didn't knowingly speak to anyone from any of the television companies present. I was therefore very surprised to learn when I returned home that one famous commentator (whom I know I didn't meet) had said on screen, when talking about the crowds present, that they had noticed that 'obviously the way to get through the crowds easily was to wear a clerical collar'. So, unbeknown to us, either I or one of my colleagues had been seen. Yes, we may not have spoken to that person, but who knows what the visible presence of the Church may have said to that person and to those who heard their comments on television?

One thing that many women are good at is to think that others aren't interested in 'little old me'. We can run ourselves down at times, underplay our importance, and demote ourselves to second- or third-class citizens. However, Jesus showed in his ministry that he especially valued such people – people who weren't considered by themselves or others as 'top dog'. He went out of his way to touch people with leprosy, to bless children, to feast with tax collectors, to point to the needs of the poor and marginalized, to talk to women. The story of Jesus is full of 'little people' who were important to him. Once we start to look carefully at the Bible, we find lots of people who go unnoticed, yet they played their part and helped shape the story of salvation – and a number of these are women.

Sometimes the biblical narrative makes them less visible: the story of Abraham, Sarah and Hagar in Genesis sees Hagar give birth to Ishmael, but then we hear little or nothing of either of them, as their original importance is eclipsed by the fact that Sarah was then able to bear a son who was called Isaac, and it is he who is often remembered first. Yet if we read on, we hear of Ishmael's sons in Genesis 25, and in Isaiah 60 we hear of the same sons sharing in the blessings of the new Jerusalem. Even though humanly their grandmother appears to be written out of the story, it seems that they can't be written out of God's love.

Sometimes it is we the readers who overlook important characters. In Exodus 2 we hear the beginnings of the story of Moses, of how he was hidden in the reeds beside the River Nile because Pharoah had decreed that all Hebrew boys should be killed at birth. Because of this, Moses shouldn't have survived and gone on to be the hugely important Bible character that he was. We know the story well, yet how often do we remember the story of Shiprah and Puah, the midwives who refused to kill Hebrew boys at birth? Without their actions, we wouldn't have had Moses, and the Hebrew people wouldn't have 'increased in number and in strength'. Likewise, many say that the pivotal point of the gospel narratives is Peter's confession that Jesus is the Messiah (Matthew 16.13–20; Mark 8.27–30; Luke 9.18–21). It is on the strength of this confession that Peter is regarded as 'the chief among the apostles' and a cornerstone of the Church; and yet, in John's Gospel, the confession that Jesus is Messiah is not made by Peter but by Martha, the sister of Mary and Lazarus (John 11.27) – the same Martha whom we often undervalue because we are more familiar with the story of

her staying at her housework rather than going to sit and listen
to Jesus' words when he visited their home (Luke 10.38–42). It
seems that around Jesus, women found freedom and equality;
yet we forget or ignore Martha's confession of faith, which is
every bit as impressive as Peter's.

It was, of course, also a woman, Mary Magdalene, who was
first to see and hear the fact of the resurrection. It was that
same woman who was sent to go and tell the disciples that their
Lord was risen. It was that same woman who proclaimed to all
who would listen, 'I have seen the Lord.' If we want to do as
Jesus did, and give everyone their full value, we would do well
to return to the biblical record, and recover the true worth of
many forgotten people, particularly women.

If by now you are thinking that I am a tub-thumping, bra-
burning feminist, I can assure you that I do not fit much of
that rather jaded stereotype. However, I am a feminist in the
sense that I see women as having an equal worth to men within
society, within sport, and within the Church. I'm also a great
believer in the complementarity of the genders. We need each
other if our communities are to function properly, and both
genders need acknowledging fully. In 1986 the Church of England produced a report called *All That Is Unseen*, followed in
1988 by another called *Making Women Visible*. In the world of
sport, the Women's Sports Foundation (WSF) have launched a
campaign to address 'the appalling gender imbalance of sports
coverage' in the UK. They say: 'The under representation of
sportswomen in the media, together with the under representation of women who bring us the news about sport has long been
a concern to those trying to increase the visibility of women's
sport.' This is supported by WSF and Sport England research
that reveals that an astoundingly low average of between 1
and 6 per cent of media coverage of UK sport is dedicated to
women. The consequence of poor media coverage is poor levels
of sponsorship, which in turn perpetuates the dearth of visible
role models, and thus the continuing invisibility of women in
sport.

The WSF campaign goes further than simply making women
more visible. It is also calling for equity in the media coverage
of women's sport, since much of the coverage that does exist is

seen as derogatory or demeaning towards women. This is either through focusing on their physical appearance, often accompanied by photographs slightly more suited to glamour magazines than sports coverage, or through commenting on their personal life or lifestyle, especially using phrases that locate them safely within female domestic traditions. For example, female athletes are often referred to as 'mother and housewife', while men are simply celebrated and turned into national heroes when they do well in sport. Some go so far as to observe that male sports stars are often disconnected from their families, because this domesticated context somehow diminishes their manly, sporting status.[10] 'Failing to highlight the athleticism, skill and achievements of our top competitors further undermines the status of women in sport', says the WSF campaign material.

As has been noted, lack of media coverage of women's sport can lead to women being seen as of less value by potential sponsors and some event organizers. This partly explains why, although elite female athletes are just as likely as male athletes to receive income from prize money, appearance money and sponsorship, such income is typically half that paid to male athletes.[11] In women's football in the UK, it is substantially less than half what the men receive! In addition, women involved in elite-level sport find access to good quality support services more difficult than men, according to Sport England's 1997 Development of Sport Talent study. This may be a generalization, but sportswomen also tend to be more concerned about financial hardship, more dependent on family support and less satisfied with access to sports science, sports medicine and good quality facilities. Other issues particularly pertinent for women in sport include sexual harassment and misunderstanding, eating disorders, and gender-specific medical issues. Of course, alongside these more gender-specific concerns, sportswomen experience the same highs and lows, the same balance between excellence and injury, the same positives and negatives, as sportsmen do, and good sports chaplains recognize, acknowledge and work with this.

Every sportsperson, of whichever gender, is an individual of great worth to God, and so should be of worth also to other human beings. We're all made with a unique personality, and

although we're all different we should all fit together and complement each other. A complement is something that completes,
matches, balances out, or supplements something else. There
will always be differences between the genders and between
individuals, in physical strength perhaps as well as in particular
skills, but both sportsmen and sportswomen train equally hard
to achieve their goals, and all are of equal worth to God. As
was said in some reflections on women in the Church, 'I do not
think that even the most conservative view of the relationship of
woman to man can escape the need for equality *and* differentia-
tion between them before God.'[12]

So, are women's football and women in sports chaplaincy
going nowhere? Although he doesn't always enamour himself
to women in football because of his sometimes sexist remarks
(such as that in 2004 when he said that female footballers
should wear skimpy clothes similar to those worn by beach
volleyball players!),[13] FIFA's general secretary Sepp Blatter did
say in 1995 that 'the future of football is feminine' and in 1996
that 'by 2010 women's football will be as important as the
men's'.[14] Although girls' and women's football is now the fast-
est growing participation sport in the UK, and in many schools
has taken over from the more traditional girls' sports of hockey
and netball, it is unlikely that his words will be fulfilled by 2010.
However, women's football is a fast-growing sport, as is demon-
strated by the 30 per cent increase in participation from 2004
to 2005 referred to earlier; and growth means more exposure,
and so more acceptance of what was termed the 'more beautiful
game' by some of the Women's Euro 2005 publicity.

Many people involved in different aspects of women's sport
believe that we are entering an exciting era in the history of
sport. The progress made by women has been significant in
recent years and, although there are still barriers to be overcome, there is great hope for the future. As women gain more
freedom to define their role and image as sportspeople, then
there should be more respect and acceptance. There are already
some sports where women compete on equal footing with
men, such as superbike, some horse races and, increasingly, a
few golf competitions, but this is not necessarily the aim for
all sports. There may always be some 'male' sports and some

'female' sports; what is yearned for is equal acceptance of both women and men as valid and professional sportspeople, and the freedom to choose which sport to be involved in.

In our society, there are many questions regarding the relationship between gender and skills, whether they be the sporting skills that make a good footballer, the pastoral skills that make an effective sports chaplain, or other skills for other roles. Although I think that there are obviously differences in approach to both sports participation and sports chaplaincy, I am of the opinion that variations are probably more due to individual personality than gender. However, I have become acutely aware, both in the Church generally and in discussions about sports chaplaincy in particular, that rather than challenge gender stereotypes, many people's opinions tend to reinforce them, even if that expressly wasn't their intention. Many say that women ministers display certain pastoral skills that men don't, while others have said that there are some things that people will talk about much more readily to a woman (even macho footballers in their most testosterone charged moments!) – subjects cited in research for this chapter include family matters, grief, 'real' reactions to injury or disappointment, and some personal medical matters. Alyson Peberdy, a social anthropologist, studied similar issues and responses in 1985 prior to the ordination of women in the Church of England. She reported:

> I found myself striving to make sense out of an apparent contradiction in what I was finding. On the one hand there was an emphasis on the similarities between women ministers and their [male] clergy colleagues . . . On the other hand many people speak of women's ministry as being different to men's.[15]

I have much sympathy with Alyson Peberdy's statement! It appears that, as much as many of us wish not to be hidebound by gender stereotypes, they are very much a part of life. The challenge is, rather than them being a straitjacket with which to restrict people, they need to be acknowledged and then used creatively as a framework to bring freedom, thus enabling each person to become and be the individual that God made them to be.

Questions are also raised as to whether sportspeople prefer a chaplain of the same gender as themselves. Although various sportsmen and sportswomen have said that a chaplain's own personal qualities would be more important than their gender, by and large women were more inclined to the view that the gender was important, some quite strongly. Perhaps this relates to shared experience of sometimes having to fight for acceptance? I don't know for certain, but it does reinforce the need for more women to be involved in sports chaplaincy alongside male ministers. What is important in all chaplaincy is that people can feel relaxed with the minister, whatever their gender, so that positive and affirming connections can be made between God and the world in which they operate. That way, we can all be going somewhere rather than nowhere.

15. You'll never walk alone

JEFFREY HESKINS
Charlton Athletic

It is little wonder that Danny Murphy was sceptical when his significant other was approached to write a column entitled, 'The Footballer's Wife' . . . 'People watch "Footballers Wives" and "Dream Team" and seriously take it in.' He shakes his head. 'Life isn't as glamorous as everyone makes out.'[1]

Reading the reflections of these chapters it might be easy to conclude that the only use anyone has for chaplains and chaplaincy in football or anywhere else are in moments of pastoral crisis. Nothing could be further from the truth. Most people are not in crisis most of the time, and that is as true of footballers and people associated with the beautiful game as anyone else. Take yourself off to a professional football stadium on any day other than a match day and it echoes rather than buzzes. Our preoccupation with what we perceive as the glitz and glamour is to some extent fuelled by the scriptwriters of soaps that Murphy identifies, but these are writers who know that their audience largely comprises of testosterone-charged young men. Theirs is often a world like a football stadium on a weekday. Too often it echoes emptily in reality and needing the fantasy buzz of a script where football, cars and women are all fast, and where life is lived frantically and on the edge. But while I am not suggesting that all players and fans lead empty lives, it is in the echoes of the weekday stadium that we find ordinary lives often needing attention.

Eugene Peterson pastored a church in North America for more than twenty years before going off to teach theology students in Canada. Whenever I read him, it is as though he has been reading me. I find myself thinking, 'How does he know that this happens to me?' The situations of pastoral ministry he describes in a way that makes me feel they are my own. He describes what he calls the 'ministry of small talk'.[2] In my own pastoral ministry I have always thought myself to have been rather good at what I reckoned was small talk, but secretly there has been a part of me that has always despised myself for it. Somehow it seems shallow and dull, and often I feel that I collude with those I spend time alongside, visiting the humdrum places of the everyday.

> Given the choice between a heated discussion on theories of the Atonement and the casual banter over the prospects of the coming Little League season, I didn't hesitate. It was the Atonement every time. If someone in the room raised questions of eschatology, it wasn't too long before I was in the thick of the talk; but if the conversation dipped to the sale of radial tires at the local dealers, my attention flagged . . . What time did I have for small talk when I was committed to the large message of salvation and eternity?[3]

I have to confess that I haven't felt his passion in quite the same way, but I know what he means, and as a consequence I have come to view the ministry of small talk in quite a different way. As a pastor and a chaplain it is so easy to want to make the starting point of the pastoral encounter where you think everyone else ought to be rather than where they are. When that happens, the loser is always the chaplain. So perhaps it is an implicit feature of chaplaincy life that we engage in the natural language that we have come disparagingly to call small talk; it is out of small talk that big opportunities arise. That is not the same as manipulating conversations from the small talk of the ordinary and everyday to the big talk of God and salvation as a way of 'witnessing'. While there may be a place for that, this is rather more a noticing where thoughtful shoots of growth are happening. It is about sowing the seed and knowing when to shut up, and if that is what is at the heart of small talk as a ministry then it is something that all forms of chaplaincy should learn to cultivate. So the ministry of small talk begins in the place where we find people, not in the place where we want to move them on to.

> If we bully people into talking on our terms, if we manipulate them into responding to our agenda, we do not take them seriously where they are in the ordinary and the everyday.
>
> Nor are we likely to become aware of the tiny shoots of green grace that the Lord is allowing to grow in the back yards of their lives. If we avoid small talk, we abandon the very field in which we have been assigned to work . . . Most of us, most of the time are engaged in simple routine tasks, and small talk is the natural language. If pastors belittle it, we belittle what most people are doing most of the time, and the gospel is misrepresented.[4]

During the summer, I experienced two examples that had the very effect of bearing out this insight. The first was at a meeting of Anglican clergy where we had agreed previously to discuss baptismal policy in our respective parish churches. Being Anglicans we all had a rather different take on the matter we commonly call 'infant baptism', more accurately known as 'the baptism of those who cannot answer for themselves'. Some of us operated an open baptism policy, offering the sacrament to any within the parish who came asking for it, while others required periods of extended preparation, and others signs of commitment to church attendance. One incumbent operated a closed policy that meant, as he told us, that baptism was not offered for children of the parish community who didn't belong to the congregational community as well. He cited the example of someone who had visited the church office earlier in the year. 'When they come to me saying that they want their child christened, I tell them that they don't really want baptism, what they really want is a naming ceremony.' When I pressed him on what had happened after this, he rather sheepishly admitted that although they had said they would go away and think about it, he had not seen them since.

The second was one that followed about two weeks later. Roger declares himself a 'confirmed atheist'. However, he comes to church to support his children on the particular Sunday we set aside to focus on the younger congregation and the church's sponsored uniformed organizations. One morning he stopped me to ask a favour. He had just finished building a boat, would I come and bless it? Of course I would, particularly when I discovered that the boatyard it was in was his back garden, a stone's throw from where I live. When I arrived on the agreed day, it was a sunny afternoon and he had invited his neighbours from the street. The boat was ready and we all admired it. The name plate was covered, the champagne was ready (for drinking – not to smash against the boat), and we had a prepared service of blessing for the boat, for her crew, for fair weather and for pleasant sailing. As we sat around sampling the champagne afterwards, one of the children asked Roger why, since he was an atheist, he wanted the boat blessed. I heard him reply that it was because he believed that ritual was important. Later, he asked me if I thought that was a satisfactory answer. I told him that I thought it was a good answer to give an 11-year-old girl, but that I hoped that long before she was 16 she would ask him just *why* he thought ritual was important and why it had been so important to do this one in this particular way. I have no idea where he has gone with that answer, but I hope that I have planted a seed that will grow into something. I have become fairly certain that Roger is not nearly the confirmed atheist he says he is because he seems to be asking too many good questions. What I am fairly sure of is that Roger is on some kind of journey into which he is more than prepared to invite people if they can meet him where he is. That was the difference in the two pastoral encounters. The first was so preoccupied with getting the couple to where the pastor wanted them to be that it simply blew up. Regardless of whatever one might feel about the issue of the baptism itself, from a pastoral perspective it seemed to me a clumsy piece of bungling. The second, by way of contrast, has kept everyone on side, given Roger space to think and be challenged by the voice of a child.

Of course, Roger is right. Ritual is very important and most of us engage in it at some level. Even if it is just to offer a handshake at a first-time meeting, we know what it means, and it usually requires no explanation. The world of football is no different, as football fans know all too well.

What happened was, Chris Roberts bought a sugar mouse from Jack Reynolds ('The Rock King'), bit its head off, dropped it in the Newmarket Road before he could get started on the body, and it got run over by a car. And that afternoon Cambridge United, who had hitherto been finding life difficult in the Second Division (two wins all season, one home, one away), beat Orient 3–1, and a ritual was born. Before each home game we all of us trooped into the sweet shop, purchased our mice, walked outside, bit the head off as though we were removing the pin from a grenade, and tossed the torsos under the wheels of oncoming cars; Jack Reynolds would stand in the doorway watching us, shaking his head sorrowfully. United, thus protected, remained unbeaten at the Abbey for months.[5]

This is one form of ritual that most football fans recognize. It is up there with all those other habits of not putting the football shirt on until you are about to go out the door, or eating a packet of crisps when the team is trailing by a goal to nil. My son berates me if I walk on any of the manhole covers on our way to the game. In the cold light of rational day we are all embarrassed to think that indulging in such absurdities can really change the course of the match to favour the team we support. But there are other forms of ritual that football clubs commonly encourage that deserve the question 'Why?'

It has become increasingly common for players to gather round the centre circle at the beginning of a match, and thousands of spectators to stand in silence for two minutes for any number of causes or events or losses. Sometimes the association of the cause is obvious. A famous player associated with the club from yesteryear has died. Sometimes the cause seems rather less obvious and might be equated with a national or international disaster. The decision to do something may be good, but what is going on, why do we do it, and why the need to do this ritual here in a football stadium? Desmond Morris has already been quoted as referring to the football stadium as the street temple, and it is not a bad image as we have already seen.[6] Ritual often serves us best in the place where we can identify. In a recent conversation with the chaplain of Manchester City, he described the moving experience of the club transporting itself from its old stadium site in Maine Road to the new City of Manchester Stadium, which had originally been built for the Commonwealth Games. In response to requests from the bereaved to the club, he offered to conduct a service for any who had particular memories associated with the old ground, emphasizing that it would be a serious event, ordered and organized and starting on time. People implicitly knew the value in this, and far from the handful that some had thought might turn out, something like a thousand people appeared for the ceremony in the old street temple of Maine Road.

But ritual is more than simply identifying with a place or an event. At best, it ought to lead the participants into a fuller understanding of whatever they are trying to grasp. In order for this to happen, good ritual needs someone to lead it. It is a sad misconception that this is a job anyone can do. I have seen countless examples, both within church and elsewhere, of this happening. A disembodied voice announcing a two-minute silence at a stadium is every bit as bad as the unimaginative drone of the verbose vicar who has to explain everything about the service as he or she goes along. Perhaps this too is where chaplains can come into their own – not simply as experts in leading the silence or the sing-along, but as those who lead a ritual in a way that enables participants to move beyond thinking that the service or the act of silence was 'quite nice' to asking some of the bigger questions of life. This is where I hope that Roger the boat-builder has been led at the moment. He has had the experience; he implicitly knows the value of ritual and has acknowledged that; but for him the question remains: what does it mean and where does it take him next in his life journey? All it has taken is for someone to meet him where he is and point him to the question that he asks on the way.

The Christian life is often described as a journey, and for me it remains one of the traditional images that continue to resonate in the contemporary era. Things often happen on journeys that turn up the unexpected. Of all the New Testament writers, my favourite exponent of the journey is Luke the evangelist and physician. In his Gospel and its bestselling sequel the Acts of the Apostles, he does this time and again, recording not only the event, but what happens on the way. Often these accounts follow a pattern. The traveller is struggling with what we might call their inner journey, an event or experience that they thought would make sense, but in fact makes none. Then there is the surprise encounter. This is followed by a moment of reflection, a new question, and then a ritual in which the participant is transformed and led in a different direction or way of thinking. Always it inspires faith.

For me, the best of these examples are found at the end of the Gospel and the beginning of the Acts. The journey to Emmaus is unique to Luke in the synoptic tradition. In it he describes two depressed and disillusioned disciples of Christ walking from Jerusalem to the village of Emmaus after the crucifixion of their inspired leader, Jesus of Nazareth.[7] A stranger joins them, and Luke tells the reader it is Jesus himself. He asks them why they are downcast; as they walk together, they explain the events of Jesus' death and their disappointment. As they continue walking away from Jerusalem, the unrecognized Jesus offers an impromptu Bible study in which he invites them to see the apparent disaster in a different way. At what they think is their journey's end they press him to stay, and in the fourfold ritual of taking, blessing, breaking and giving bread, their eyes are opened and they see the whole situation in a different light. They do a U-turn and make their way back to Jerusalem, transformed.

Similarly in Acts, Luke treats us to the colourful story of the Ethiopian eunuch, again travelling away from Jerusalem having been on pilgrimage.[8] Myra Blyth suggests that his pilgrimage might well have been a frustrating journey fuelled by his curiosity, but in which, on his arrival at Jerusalem, would have been compounded by his exclusion from visiting anything other than the outer courts of the Temple.[9] It is almost as if he might have gone to the tourist shop and bought a copy of the scroll containing Isaiah 53 to pass the time on the way home. But as he makes the journey, he is met by the unexpected figure of Philip who helps him make connections with the passage he is reading and struggling to understand. As they journey together, Philip helps the Ethiopian see that there is another way of looking at God. He invites him to see how the image of the suffering servant makes God appear both vulnerable and accessible. Here

God can be seen as one who knows what it is to be rejected and turned away. This is certainly something that would ring bells for the Ethiopian, perhaps feeling rejected by his Temple experience in his search for God. Even when they reach the water, there is a note of uncertainty in his question, 'What is to prevent me being baptized?' It is as if he half expects that there will be further rejection. Then the ritual of baptism is administered, the Ethiopian realizes the transformation, and he continues the journey without Philip, no longer baffled and frustrated by rejection, but rejoicing.

In both of these stories the pastoral figure enables the disappointed, rejected, frustrated figures to see things in a different way, and the act of ritual becomes a symbolic participation in that changed reality. We began this book with an image of the chaplain as guardian of the sacred, but it seems to me that this figure has evolved into something more intricate than a mere protector of sacred space. What appears to be emerging from these chapters now is a development of that image into one that is more subversive. Perhaps it is part of our task to recognize the potential for, and help create something sacred in, what has hitherto been regarded as secular space. If it is, then this is nothing terribly new; it is something that has undergone a latter-day revival in the re-emergence of Celtic worship and spirituality.

Long before Roman Christianity established itself in Britain, the Christian faith had been kept by Celtic Britons for some centuries, for we know that as early as the Council of Arles in 314 British bishops were present. However, the arrival of the mission under Augustine from Rome in about 596 saw the beginning of tension between two quite different cultures and expressions of the Christian religion. The Celts were something of a loose configuration of Christians who seemed to hold together as a federation of local churches sharing good will. The culture was predominantly rural; they were not prone to keeping written records, and the stories of their communities were passed on from memory. By way of contrast, the Roman Christians under Augustine emerged from an urban context with a culture to match. They were organized and literate and prone to setting down roots that established the characteristics of their culture and faith in the most distinct way. They were for settling down and drawing everyone into line. It was inevitable that the two systems would eventually collide, and collide they did in 664 at the Synod of Whitby. Ostensibly it was about agreeing and fixing the date of Easter, so that it might be universally observed, or so the Venerable Bede would have us believe.[10] However, Bede is clearly dismissive of the Celts, describing Bishop Finan of Lindisfarne as 'A hot tempered man whom reproof made more obstinate and openly hostile to the truth.'[11] It is clear this is a perspective of the Synod so laced with bias as to suggest this was really a power struggle over which group was going to run the Church. Bede, the good Roman Christian that he is, tells us that the Catholicism of the Roman missionaries won the day and established the ordering of Christianity as we now know it. Since the Celts never wrote any records, we have only his word for it!

Historically, the Church has often preoccupied itself with winning the argument – whether that argument has been over the divine nature of Christ in its early years, justification by faith through grace in the Reformation period, or the sex and gender issues that have coloured the present era. In many ways I think it is a shame not to have learned other lessons from Whitby's Celtic and Roman participants. It seems to me that each represents a dynamic of Christian faith that can only be properly held in tension in the presence of the other; the Romans representing a much-valued settled centre and the Celts that of dynamic movement. I think that it is no accident that the current renaissance of Celtic spirituality and liturgy has emerged at the same time as the growth and development of chaplaincy in so many walks of life.

Most of us who are engaged in the work of chaplaincy at football clubs know about the need to hold this tension. We are regarded as members of the football club's staff, yet none of us is in its pay. Most of us therefore find ourselves either running a local church or on the staff of one. Anyone who has found themselves in such a ministry knows that running a local church can of itself be all-absorbing, even with a plentiful supply of volunteers or paid staff. Maintaining and administering the settled centre is important work, but it needs the challenges that the opportunities of dynamic movement bring. God never calls us to a ministry of self-absorption, but as we journey like the Emmaus disciples and the Ethiopian official back and forth between the places of the settled centre and those of dynamic movement we might find ourselves engaging in the ministry of subversion – an important and often overlooked feature of chaplaincy life.

Whatever legacy the Celts left, theirs was certainly one that had immense respect for starting where people were and not where others might like them to be. St Columba and his followers adopted this principle in all their mission work.[12] They held open-air worship and transformed what they found without destroying what it had previously been. So when Columbanas, a later follower of Columba, came across a ruined temple to the goddess Diana in France, he had it restored and used it as the church for his new monastery. All of this was possible because of the Celtic understanding that God was already at work in a place long before they ever got there. It is a humbling spirituality, but one which gives a perspective on human living that helps us understand the ministry of subversion for what it really is, and not what it is often mistaken to be.

Subversion, ordinarily understood, is one of those words that suggest the destruction of an authority or ideology. Often it is depicted as the possession of the trusted who have finally revealed themselves as the treacherous. We see it as dramatic in its activity and devastating in its result. But there is another feature of subversion that is nothing like that. Sometimes, subversion can be like the movement that is erosion. It happens quietly and effects the state of change quite unconsciously. The very nature of pastoral ministry itself is prone to subversion, as anyone running a church will tell you.

> In running a church I solve problems. Wherever two or three are gathered together, problems develop. Egos are bruised, procedures get snarled, arrangements become confused, plans go awry . . . The difficulty is that problems arrive in such a constant flow that problem solving becomes full time work. Because it is useful and the pastor ordinarily does it well, we fail to see that the pastoral vocation has been subverted.[13]

And so it needs to be rescued, which ironically I am suggesting can be done in a theological 'homeopathic' way. Ordinarily, the curative nature of medicine is to attack the illness with its opposite. Homeopathy is the cure of like with like. The gift of the Celts to the world of chaplaincy is the gift of theological subversion. If our pastoral ministry is being subverted at the centre, then let's use the tool of subversion as we are now trying to understand it to make the rescue. If chaplains are simply defined in the benign language that they are good to have around because they are well practised at problem-solving or being nice to people and no more than that, then the whole notion of chaplaincy is rendered harmless. Who wants to live like that? If instead we can subvert the benign image of chaplaincy and take it to a different place where those same people can be challenged through it without being threatened by it, then subversion need not be seen as destructive, but something that always looks positively towards change and transformation. How do we go about it? Well, maybe we need to mind our language. This is what I mean.

We often lament that the cultural context we inhabit in Western Europe and North America is overwhelmingly secular. While that may be a correct assessment, it is something that we would do better to meet the challenge of than lament. My own experience suggests that in such a context chaplains are a paradox. We seem not to fit the context and yet the context allows us a place within it. When I read the Gospels in order to build a picture of Jesus of Nazareth, I see that, in one sense, it is no different now to then.

I don't much like the image of religious minister as I often experience it. We occupy an odd niche and I sit very uneasily with the caricature of the pastor as a somewhat harmless innocent, fondly regarded but not a serious player in the game of life. In church we speak a language so very much at odds with the everyday experiences of our congregations, who then return to what one once advised me was the 'real world'. Sometimes it leaves me feeling quite marginal and surplus to requirements. Like many, I often confuse being valued with being important. At my worst, I claim that I want to be taken seriously, but what I confuse is the seriousness of the subversive way of life I try to live out (value) and the trap of taking myself seriously (importance). When I look at the Gospels, religious leaders then, as now, seem to suffer the same pitfalls. Rabbis were accorded respect and many of them demanded it, but they don't seem to make much happen. Yet Jesus, who allows himself to be called Rabbi, does, and he does it by adopting the language of the cultural context in which he finds himself.

> Jesus' favourite speech form, the parable, was subversive. Parables sound absolutely ordinary: casual stories about soil and seeds, meals and coins and sheep, bandits and victims, farmers and merchants. And they are wholly secular: of his forty or so parables recorded in the Gospels, only one has its setting in church, and only a couple mention the name God.[14]

This is the language of subversive transformation. Jesus, as storyteller throws down sometimes quite odd stories alongside ordinary lives and then does nothing. He uses the language of the everyday, the images of the familiar and the examples of the things that are around him, to challenge people in their own time. It is subversive without being destructive. His stories don't illustrate, they demand thinking about in order that those hearing them might think again about the bigger picture of life. Those who wrote these stories down at the end of his earthly life grasped the point right away. They called them 'gospels', now a wholly religious word, but then a secular one, the same word that was used to describe an imperial political manifesto.[15] Even the term 'gospel' was subversive! Seen this way, chaplains should never take themselves seriously or demand the same from those they live and work among. This is not about prestige. However, we should never forget the seriousness of the mystery that we carry and that we invite others to enter into. That is the perpetual nature of what it means to be engaged in these sorties from the centre to the edges and meeting people where they are.

This has not been a book about footballers' lives. Everyone who wrote for it was agreed that this was not where they wanted to focus. There is plenty of that kind of spotlighting elsewhere and we seem to live in an age where the maintenance

of confidentiality is prized much less than the eagerness to pub-
lish memoirs that trivialize the lives of those in that spotlight.
Instead, it is a book in which football itself is the context, and
while it may be fair to say that the game itself has remained
relatively unaltered throughout its history, much of life in and
around football has changed. John Motson rightly highlights
this shift in his Foreword. When winning seems to have become
the all-important focus for the modern game, other things get
pushed out. Driven by the need for economic success, pressure
mounts at every level of club life. On the pitch a single mistake
by a player might mean the difference between one point or
three. Does that constitute a loss of form? Will they be picked
next time? A single refereeing error might make the difference between survival in the top flight and relegation. To err
is human, but that decision might make the difference between
who remains on the staff the following season and who has to
be made redundant. There are wide discrepancies in the pay
scales, with some players at the highest level often receiving as
much in a week or a month as an ancillary worker in a year.
Marketing departments have to turn in profits, ticket sales have
to remain buoyant; every aspect of life is affected. Then there
are the issues that percolate into wider society: violent conduct,
racist and sexist abuse, inclusion of those with physical disabili-
ties. These are lives built around footballing success. These are
footballing lives, but do they have to be lives that perpetuate
the culture of 'we are the champions, no time for losers'? Here
I think chaplains must come into their own.

When in 1982 as Prime Minister, Margaret Thatcher, having
dispatched the Task Force to the Falkland Islands, was asked
by a reporter what would happen in the event of failure, I seem
to remember her retort went something along the lines, 'Failure? The possibilities do not exist!' While it may have been
politically expedient to have made so robust an announcement,
it was patently untrue. In every human action made with whatever degree of faith, the possibility of failure does exist, as does
success. It is all part of what it means to be human. We all like
to succeed. Often we measure our confidence in terms of the
things that mark us as successful. There is nothing wrong in
that, but any society or institution that nurtures its need for

success without paying due regard to what happens when things go wrong is in serious danger. That danger lies in idolizing success as a culture and ignoring the human need to deal with failure when it presents itself. 'It would be extremely odd if such a profoundly human activity as pastoral care were not shot through with failure. But ultimately perhaps the real tragedy of failure lies in its being ignored, glossed over or disguised.'[16] For me this has something of the ring of truth about it. The possibilities for failure always exist and present themselves in diverse ways, as we have seen already in the preceding chapters. The sense of failure that receivership evokes; the feelings of failing to graduate beyond the youth academy; or the sense of failing to recover from injury are all real, but too often they are stories that are hidden because we do not allow ourselves the means of dealing with them.

If colluding with the culture of success has meant ultimately that in some respects we have lost our perspective on life, then we need to recover it, and clearly, as previous chapters also identify, there are instances when that has been so. Players at the peak of their careers face the tragedy that is the end of their playing days and look for life beyond football. Clubs on the edge of extinction rise from the ashes. A child facing loss and grief finds comfort in the unexpected kindness of a personal initiative. The ministry of subversion as I have described it is only subversive when it eventually allows those meeting it a chance to see the values that it espouses. For Christians, these emerge in the form that the Gospels describe as the Kingdom of God. This Kingdom is not a territory or a piece of land, but an entire way of looking at life from a different point of view. The Gospels tell us that this is the way that God views the world. They are subversive values in which the last will be first and the first last; where the mighty will be humbled and the humble exalted. At a personal level they emerge as a pastoral care package that extols the virtues of patience, kindness, goodness, tenderness, gentleness and self-discipline. St Paul makes a lot of these virtues for community living. At a prophetic level they speak boldly of the need for justice and fairness and for those who think they have power and influence now to take a second look at how human and vulnerable they really are.

Entering into the pain of failure appears to be entry into a dark place. It is the mystery of our human nature. We simply don't know why these things happen in human life, but they force us to move on from the futile question of why this happened to me, to the bigger question of what I know about myself now that I didn't know before, and where it takes me on my life journey. Where can chaplains be in that? Well, perhaps they can move on from the rather dull image of the ever-pleasant problem-solver to that of the more challenging travelling companion within the mystery of life.

Alan Hansen, the former Liverpool footballer and now television match analyst, has produced and fronted a documentary for the BBC looking at how players cope with the end of their playing careers.[17] Most of those interviewed had been fortunate enough to have full playing careers and in that sense none of them could have described their life in football as a failure, but each of them had dealt with the prospect of life after football quite differently. Some had made contingency plans, but most had struggled to avoid the agony of facing the end. They simply didn't know how to leave the game they had served as a player. In the final shot, Hansen is seen walking the touchline on the pitch at Anfield where he had played and will have heard countless times the fans of the Kop end singing, 'You'll never walk alone'. As he looks up he concludes: 'Is it good out here? Well, it's a journey . . . and there's no going back.'

Perhaps our biggest failure is in not letting those footballing lives know that there are some parts of the journey that they need not make alone. That is the perennial challenge to a meaningful and purposeful chaplaincy in a success-driven culture where the prospect of failing is debilitating largely because of the fear it induces. If chaplains have understood that there is no status in their chaplaincy they will be in a position to challenge this fear when they meet it in others. If they themselves remain unresolved in this, they will not only be unhelpful, they might even inadvertently be the cause of harm. The values of the Kingdom that we all need to underpin our Christian ministries will inform us of this, for the prominent idea of success is not one to be found in the Gospels. In fact it has only become prominent in western society quite recently. For someone like

Shakespeare, success was a way of describing progress. It was, if you like, a manner in which one could plot personal growth. This is something that the admirable Jean Vanier took up and accorded equally to the whole notion of failure: 'In questions pertaining to life, there is no real success, only growth. I believe that I have learned more through my mistakes and failures than through the successes.'[18]

Chaplains, particularly in football clubs, need to be able to say amen to that for themselves and sit with it when they encounter it in others. It needs to be done not least of all because it is a difficult thing for any of us to do. Ministers, priests and chaplains in particular are as prone to insecurity as anyone. Most of us look for and need the love and approval of those among whom we work. We like to be liked, and there is no shame in that; but the call to an authentic subversive ministry can be at personal cost.

Chapter 1 concluded with the image of Geoffrey Studdert Kennedy transforming the nature of chaplaincy through his experience of the filth and futility that was the failure of war in the trenches during 1914–18. His subversion lay in his reflection on what it meant to enter the darkness of that failure. Those reflections were not only a prophetic challenge to the establishment figures of his day; they made him ask questions of himself and thus see his ministry as one bound up with those he ministered to. His was no patronizing work of a superior with all the answers; rather the opposite. Kennedy gained no preferment or reward from the establishment for this. It seems to me that chaplaincy is nothing at all if it doesn't make all chaplains ask themselves those self-same questions. Why am I doing this? What is it all about? What am I learning about me in this encounter? How can I take those insights into the ministry of pastoral care God has entrusted to me? This kind of reflection on practice is both honest and liberating. 'If you have come to help me, then you are wasting your time. But if you have come because your liberation is bound up with mine, then let us work together.'[19]

If the task is to see that nobody ever has to walk alone on the journey, and that listening and commentating and helping each other interpret what we see and hear in the realities of life while we are on the way is all part of that, chaplains may just have arrived at the beginning of an important dimension of ministry in the world of footballing lives. 'In the end, the thing that Christian ministry distinctively has to offer people is not good works or righteous actions, but a way of seeing reality: "To contemplate is to *see*, and to minister is to make *visible*." '[20]

16. When the saints go marching in

MATT BAKER
Charlton Athletic

One of the best things I remember about growing up in the 1970s and '80s was the number of football comics and comic strips on the market. I wonder how many youngsters dashed to the newsagent each week to pick up the latest issue of *Tiger* or *Roy of the Rovers* to read whether Roy Race had scored the crucial goal to save Melchester Rovers from relegation, or to glean tips from the tales of the table-top heroes, *Mike's Mini Men*, in the days when subbuteo filled the imagination gap before the advent of fantasy leagues. Yet, of all these, my personal favourite was *Billy's Boots*, which began life in *Scorcher*. Billy Dane was the proud owner of a pair of old-fashioned football boots previously owned by the 1920s ace Dead Shot Keen. Without these boots Billy was useless, but when he wore the boots of the former goal-scoring legend his game was transformed and he found himself the star of his school team.

As I write the concluding thoughts to this book, and read over the contributions from fellow chaplains, I am reminded once more of Billy's exploits. On many occasions he would find himself ghosting into the opponents' penalty area, or drifting out to the wing, without any idea as to why he was there, or, perhaps more significantly, *how* he got there. Suddenly, as if from nowhere, the ball would land at his feet, and before he knew what was happening he had beaten two or three players and rifled the ball into the back of the net. As he was mobbed by his team mates and bathed in the glory, a bubble would appear in the comic strip as Billy pondered the real reason for his success: 'Is this me or Dead Shot Keen?'

As chaplains, we never get mobbed and rarely receive any of the glory, which is as it should be since it is neither the aim of chaplaincy nor the role of the chaplain. However, many, if not all of us, have found ourselves at our football clubs in situations that we have not engineered and can't really explain, yet which achieve something of importance in the lives of those we minister to. Every week as I drive to Charlton's training ground, I pray to be filled with the Holy Spirit and ask God to open my eyes to what he is doing so that I might join in with it. The rest is then up to him, and he never seems to disappoint.

In Chapter 2, John Boyers has written of the early days of football chaplaincy spawned by a conversation with Mike Pusey one Saturday back in 1977. Few would have known then the extent to which this would grow over the next thirty years. Chaplaincy is now operating within more than seventy of the ninety-two Premiership, Championship and League clubs.

Each chaplaincy in detail is different, depending on a variety of factors, including the amount of time the chaplain has to give, the size of the club involved, the openness of the playing and administration sides to chaplaincy, and the past work this chaplain or a previous chaplain has done in the club. Added to this of course are the different strengths and personalities of the chaplains involved. However, in more recent years, SCORE has tried to define just what is meant by a 'chaplaincy involvement'. A code of practice has been drawn up, which seeks to define the parameters and responsibilities of the chaplain, the club and the charity. The aim is to provide excellence and professionalism in chaplaincy services to sport, and to work hard in identifying potential new chaplains who will deliver a quality service and commend the whole concept of chaplaincy.

Developments have come out of the foundational work in football and entered many other sporting contexts, including rugby league, rugby union, county cricket, athletics and horse racing, where, since 2000, SCORE's Director of Horse Racing Chaplaincy, Graham Locking, has worked to pioneer chaplaincy. There are also further SCORE regional representatives working across the UK, and, as detailed in Chapter 14, Mary Vickers was appointed in 2005 as Chaplaincy Co-ordinator for Women in Sport. Additionally, as chaplaincy has been recognized in different sports, there has been involvement in setting up, organizing and supervising chaplaincy provision at various major sports events, most significantly being the recent work at the 2002 Manchester Commonwealth Games and the 2004 Athens Olympics and Paralympics.

It is clear that the journey of chaplaincy has already covered some distance and continues to grow. But this book has not just been about the length of the journey; it has also emphasized how chaplaincy is about being called alongside others in the journey. Just like Woodbine Willie of the First World War, there have been many examples of chaplains being drawn in and alongside those on their own journey. Some have found this by simply being there, or by playing an instrumental role in the formation of Supporters' Trusts, crucial to a club's survival. Others, whether in the physio room or strolling around a football pitch, find themselves there 'for such a time as this', however brief, developing relationships and offering a listening ear at moments of significance in an individual's life.

It doesn't take much time in theological reflection to understand where the impetus for this comes from. Like the bubble of thought in *Billy's Boots*, I often find myself wondering about the influential activity of the Holy Spirit, who comes alongside. In fact perhaps the third person of the Trinity is a very good way to understand the involvement of a chaplain. Always there, but not always perceived. Enigmatic and hard to define, yet pervasive and at times persuasive. Understood to be there as a comforter, in the sense of listening and helping to soothe – 'Ah yes, I feel better having spoken to you, Rev' but also playing the comforter in a more subversive sense. The great Bayeux Tapestry includes a panel in which King William and his brother Bishop Odo seem to be losing the battle, but in which William is shown waving his sword around, poking and provoking his own soldiers and Odo waving his episcopal staff at the squires. Underneath, the caption translates something like, 'Bishop Odo and King William comfort the troops'.

This is a less-well-known understanding of what it means to comfort, but it makes sense when describing the Holy Spirit as the Comforter (as Jesus does in the Fourth Gospel). To comfort is indeed to be gentle, to listen and to provide space in the pastoral encounter, but it is also about being the one who encourages to the point of being provocative. Most of us see the former, but need to be challenged by the latter. I also think that this takes place in a similar way to the parables of the New Testament where listeners and readers are drawn in by their apparent familiarity only to be challenged and provoked by the punchline. This may not be the deliberate intention of those of us who are chaplains, but if we find our empowerment from the Holy Spirit we then cannot but find ourselves ministering in such a way, gentle but encouraging and sometimes challenging. The ministry of subversion (see Chapter 15) is only subversive when it eventually allows those meeting it a chance to see the values that it espouses.

Such an encounter may indeed take some time to filter through into an individual's awareness. This might be years later, perhaps after transferring to another club or even with a change in career. Nevertheless, when realization comes, subversion has taken place. I am always encouraged when I introduce myself to a new member of staff and am greeted with warmth and a smile. This usually means that they have encountered chaplaincy at a previous club and have had favourable experiences. Similarly, when I am contacted years later by a former player seeking advice or wanting to tell me something, I know that such subversion has brought some form of conversion.

From the perspective of the journey I am sure I am not the only one to observe the lack of closure offered within the world of football; a player can be at one club one week and employed by another the next. I witnessed firsthand the sense of bereavement experienced by one member of the non-playing staff who learnt that the reason they hadn't seen a particular player for a day or so was because he had moved on in the most recent transfer window. Most of us are aware in life of the importance of closure for our psychological well-being, yet it is all too easy for fans to be critical of a new signing who has 'never really done it for us'. To an extent, this will always be a necessary evil within the ever-changing football industry, but hopefully the chaplain can help bridge the gap and resolve some of the anxiety experienced. The continuity offered here and the handing over of pastoral care can play a crucial role in resettling as the journey continues in a different location.

And finally it is about our journey too. *Footballing Lives* isn't just about those we come into contact with at our football clubs; it is also about our lives within football. Hopefully a chaplain never creates a sense of 'us and them' in his or her role. We journey as well; we are formed and transformed by our on-going experiences in the journey. Chaplaincy has changed over the years, and so also have the chaplains as individuals. Alan Comfort (and given my earlier definition, what an apposite surname that is) writes in this book from a unique perspective. He is one whose journey seems to have come full circle in terms of location and who can operate more in empathy than sympathy from his own transition from player to chaplain. Yet we are all engaged in our own journey.

Football and chaplaincy continue at such a pace that we have to force ourselves to stop and reflect on what is going on. We need to create the space to contemplate the questions raised in Chapter 15; for those of us involved in writing this book I hope this has enabled us to do this. Every chaplain needs to note how the pastoral situation affects them too. What is happening? How does it make me feel? Why do I feel that way? What have I learned about God? What have I learned about myself? What difference has it made in me? Where do I go from here? I know from a personal perspective my engagement within football has challenged and sustained my faith, as well as increased my self-awareness. I recall the occasion a few years ago when someone asked me how *I* was, rather than the other way round, and pointed out that they were concerned with how stressed I was looking. This led to some discussions among the players as to whether the chaplain was supposed to be the one with everything sorted or whether it meant that at least I was human! Whatever conclusions were drawn, the significance for me was that something had changed in terms of relationships and the journey. I was also on a journey; I could allow such a conversation to inform and instruct me, and continue whatever process was at work in and through me.

I don't know how *Billy's Boots* ends. *Roy of the Rovers* as a comic ceased to exist years ago. Maybe Dead Shot's boots finally wore out, or perhaps there was a closing scene where Billy throws them in the bottom of his cupboard and concentrates his life on more 'serious' matters. But the romantic in me likes to think that somewhere out there, in some obscure publication, he is still playing week in week out, drifting into inexplicable positions and performing footballing miracles.

Back in the world of reality, those of us who have the privilege to serve as chaplains at football clubs are convinced that our journey is far from over. Football continues to grow and exert an influence on a worldwide scale, and as I write it is the turn of the year when once more teams from around the world, watched by millions in every continent, will compete for World Cup glory. Few who watch those games will be aware of the existence of chaplaincy within football, but perhaps having read this book a few more are awake to the value of such a role.

Postscript

If you have any questions relating to any aspect of the work or ministry of SCORE, please feel free to make contact through the website (www.scorechaplaincy.org.uk), or at the Watford address or phone number: SCORE, PO Box 123, Watford WD17 1LY (01923 243245).

Notes

Foreword

1 John Boyers, *Beyond the Final Whistle*, Hodder & Stoughton, 2000, p. viii.

1 Who are you, who are you?

1 Nick Hornby, *Fever Pitch*, Indigo, 1992, p. 22.
2 John King, *The Football Factory*, Vintage, 1997.
3 Hornby, *Fever Pitch*, quoting Ed Horton in the fanzine *When Saturday Comes*, p. 97.
4 *Dream Team* is a seasonal soap found only on Sky television, which depicts the fortunes of a mythological football club in the Midlands.
5 John Ayto, *Bloomsbury Dictionary of Word Origins*, Bloomsbury Publishing, 1990, p. 107.
6 Benjamin Hoff, *The Tao of Pooh*, Magnet, 1984, p. 100.
7 Alistair Campbell, *Rediscovering Pastoral Care*, Darton, Longman & Todd, 1981, pp. 47–8.
8 Acts 17.18.
9 John 19.1ff.
10 Campbell, *Rediscovering Pastoral Care*, p. 59.
11 G. A. Studdert Kennedy, *Rhymes*, Hodder & Stoughton, 1929, p. 9.
12 Robert Ellis, 'Studdert Kennedy: Poet, Pastor, Pastoral Theologian'; work in progress, paper given at the British and Irish Association for Pastoral Theology, Edinburgh, 2005.
13 Pink Floyd, 'Another Brick in the Wall'.
14 Nicholas Holtam, 'A vicar learns from Sinatra', *Church Times*, 8 July 2005, p. 24.

2 We can see you sneaking in

1 See Chapter 4 below.

3 Shall we sing a song for you?

1 Psalm 137.1, 3–4
2 See further, Alan MacDonald, *Never Walk Alone*, Hodder & Stoughton, 1994, pp. 67ff.
3 Genesis 50.19.

4 By far the greatest team

1 John 10.10.
2 Mark 5.21–34.
3 Luke 19.1–10.
4 Mark 6.30–44.

8 Who ate all the pies?

1 Jimmy Armfield, *The Autobiography – Right Back to the Beginning*, Headline, 2004, p. 136.
2 Armfield, *The Autobiography*, p. 137.
3 Norman Hunter, *Biting Talk*, Hodder & Stoughton, 2004, pp. 82f.
4 Leo McKinstry, *Jack and Bobby*, Collins Willow, 2002, p. 288.
5 Niall Quinn, *Niall Quinn: The Autobiography*, Headline, 2002, p. 190.
6 Andrew Flintoff, *Being Freddie*, Hodder & Stoughton, 2005, p. 119.
7 Genesis 1.27.
8 Patrick Barclay, *Daily Telegraph*, 4 January 2004.
9 Armfield, *The Autobiography*, p. 193.
10 Quinn, *Niall Quinn*, p. 189.
11 Hunter Davies, *Boots, Balls and Haircuts*, Cassell Illustrated, 2003, p. 243.
12 McKinstry, *Jack and Bobby*, p. 94.
13 'My God, my God, why have you forsaken me?' Matthew 27.46 (NIV).
14 Mark Nesti, *Existential Psychology and Sport: Theory and Application*, Routledge, 2006.

9 You only sing when you're winning

1 Rudyard Kipling, 'If'.
2 Brendan Batson, previously employed by the Professional Footballers' Association and now a consultant for the Football Association, in a talk given at Lilleshall National Sports Centre, 5 October 2005.
3 See Chapter 13.

4 David J. Atkinson and David H. Field (eds.), *New Dictionary of Christian Ethics and Pastoral Theology*, InterVarsity Press, 1995, p. 78.

5 Warren W. Wiersbe, *On Being a Servant of God*, Baker Books, 1993, p. 82.

6 John 1.14 (NIV).

7 Matthew 8.23–27.

8 See Chapter 1 above.

9 Screened on BBC1 on 13 May 2005.

10 Sporting Chance is a clinic that helps sportsmen overcome addictions.

11 See Chapter 11 below.

12 Tony Adams, with Ian Ridley, *Addicted*, HarperCollins, 1999, p. 290.

13 M. Robinson (ed.), *Chambers 21ˢᵗ Century Dictionary*, Chambers, 1999, p. 1409.

14 1 Corinthians 1.23–25 (NIV).

15 Harry Ricketts, *The Unforgiving Minute: A Life of Rudyard Kipling*, Chatto & Windus, 1999, p. 294.

16 Chapter 1 above.

10 Going down; going down; going down

1 David Conn, *The Beautiful Game? Searching for the Soul of Football*, Yellow Jersey Press, 2005.

2 Nick Hornby, *Fever Pitch*, Indigo, 1992, pp. 24–28.

3 The history of these events is catalogued in a publication produced by the York City Supporters' Trust, *At the Heart of the Community: Building Trust between Community and Club*, Maxiprint, November 2003.

4 Chris Titley, 'They're selling the fans down the river', *York Evening Press*, 9 January 2002.

5 York City match day programme, 29 March 2003 (issue 22), p. 8.

11 You're supposed to be at home

1 Rick Everitt, 'Battle for The Valley', *Voice of The Valley*, 1991, pp. 5–6.

2 Malcolm Torry, *Managing God's Business*, Ashgate, 2005, pp. 34ff., offers a good overview of this discussion.

3 Andrew Yip, 'The Self as the Basis of Religious Faith' in *Predicting Religion: Christian, Secular and Alternative Futures*, ed. Grace Davie, Paul Heelas and Linda Woodhead, Ashgate, 2003, pp. 1379.

4 Desmond Morris, *The Soccer Tribe*, Jonathan Cape, 1981, and quoted in Everitt, 'Battle for The Valley', p. v.
5 Sam Bartram, *Sam Bartram – By Himself*, Burke Publishing, 1956, pp. 110–12.

12 You're not singing any more

1 Richard made his debut at Derby on 29 October 1994. Evidence of his impact on the team can be seen in his being voted, in his debut year, Player of the Year by the fans and Young Player of the Year by the management.
2 John 14.6.

14 Nowhere; you're always going nowhere

1 *A Brief History of Female Football Fans* (Football Factsheet No. 9), University of Leicester, Centre for the Sociology of Sport, 2004 (available online from: http://www.le.ac.uk/so/css/resources/factsheets/index.html).
2 *Women and Football* (Football Factsheet No. 5), University of Leicester, Centre for the Sociology of Sport, 2002 (available online from: http://www.le.ac.uk/so/css/resources/factsheets/index.html).
3 Figures from the FA – personal communication.
4 Sue Lopez, *Women on the Ball*, Scarlet Press, 1997, p. 2.
5 Lopez, *Women on the Ball*, p. 193.
6 Malcolm Boyden, 'Flying the Flag for Equality', *The Times*, 10 October 2005.
7 Quoted in Lopez, *Women on the Ball*, p. 9.
8 Lopez, *Women on the Ball*, p. 23.
9 'Bridge of thighs', *Guardian*, 16 May 1977, quoted in Lopez, *Women on the Ball*, p. 83.
10 *Women and Football* (Football Factsheet No. 5), University of Leicester, Centre for the Sociology of Sport, 2002 (available online from: http://www.le.ac.uk/so/css/resources/factsheets/index.html).
11 British Olympic Association Athletes' Commission 2000.
12 Christina Baxter, 'Women in the Church: Some Personal Reflections on 1985–2000', *Crucible* (January–March 2001), p. 15 (emphasis in original).
13 Marcus Christenson and Paul Kelso, 'Soccer chief's plan to boost the women's game: Hotpants', *Guardian*, 16 January 2004.
14 Lopez, *Women on the Ball*, pp. 237 and 218 respectively.
15 Alyson S. Peberdy, *A Part of Life*, Movement for the Ordination of Women, 1985, p. 14.

15 You'll never walk alone

1 Amy Lawrence, 'Valley is Perfect for Murphy to Take Starring Role', *Observer*, 18 September 2005.

2 Eugene H. Peterson, *The Contemplative Pastor*, Eerdmans, 1993, p. 112.

3 Peterson, *The Contemplative Pastor*, p. 113.

4 Peterson, *The Contemplative Pastor*, p. 115.

5 Nick Hornby, *Fever Pitch*, Indigo, 1992, pp. 109–10.

6 Desmond Morris, *The Soccer Tribe*, Jonathan Cape, 1981, referred to in Chapter 11.

7 Luke 24.13–35.

8 Acts 8.26–39.

9 Myra Blyth, 'Theology of Chaplaincy', a keynote address given to the Annual Football Chaplains Conference, Lilleshall, 30 September 2003.

10 Bede, *A History of the English Church and People*, Dorset Press, 1985, pp. 185ff.

11 Bede, *A History*, p. 186.

12 Chris King, *Our Celtic Heritage*, St Andrew Press, 1997, pp. 27ff.

13 Peterson, *The Contemplative Pastor*, p. 64.

14 Peterson, *The Contemplative Pastor*, p. 32.

15 Ched Myers, *Binding the Strong Man*, Orbis, 1988, p. 11.

16 Stephen Pattison, *A Critique of Pastoral Care*, SCM Press, 1993, p. 158.

17 Alan Hansen, *Life After Football*, BBC1 documentary, screened 13 May 2005.

18 Jean Vanier, *Man and Woman He Made Them*, Darton, Longman & Todd, 1985, p. 4.

19 Lilla Watson, quoted in *Bread of Tomorrow*, ed. Janet Morley, SPCK/Christian Aid, 2004, p. 4.

20 Pattison, *A Critique of Pastoral Care*, p. 191, quoting Henri J. M. Nouwen, *Clowning in Rome*, Doubleday, 1979, p. 88.